Taxcafe.co.uk Tax Guides

Tax Planning for Couples

By Carl Bayley BSc ACA

Important Legal Notices

Taxcafe.co.uk tax guides are published by Taxcafe UK Limited, 214 High Street, Kirkcaldy.
Tel: (01592) 560081
Email address: team@taxcafe.co.uk

First Edition   November 2005

ISBN 1 904608 32 9

Copyright

Trademarks

Disclaimer
Before reading or relying on the content of this Tax Guide, please read carefully the disclaimer on the last page which applies. If you have queries then please contact the publisher at team@taxcafe.co.uk.

About the Author

Carl Bayley is the author of a number of tax guides designed specifically for the layman. Carl's particular speciality is his ability to take the weird, complex and inexplicable world of taxation and set it out in the kind of clear, straightforward language that taxpayers themselves can understand. As he often says himself, "my job is to translate tax into English".

Carl takes the same approach when speaking on taxation, a role he has undertaken with some relish on a number of occasions, including his highly acclaimed series of seminars at the London Property Investor Show. He has also talked about tax on BBC radio and television and, more recently, he has appeared on Irish television too.

A Chartered Accountant by training, Carl began his professional life in 1983 in the Birmingham office of one of the 'Big 4' accountancy firms. He qualified as a double prize-winner and immediately began specialising in taxation.

After 17 years honing his skills with major firms, Carl began the new millennium in January 2000 by launching his own Edinburgh-based tax consultancy practice, Bayley Consulting, through which he now provides advice on a wide variety of UK taxation issues, especially matters affecting small and medium-sized businesses and their owners, as well as property taxation and Inheritance Tax planning.

As well as being Taxcafe.co.uk's Senior Consultant, Carl is also Chairman of the Institute Members in Scotland group and a former member of the governing Council of the Institute of Chartered Accountants in England and Wales.

When he isn't working, Carl takes on the equally taxing challenges of hill walking and writing poetry.

Dedications

At its heart, this book is, of course, about relationships. It seems appropriate, therefore, for me to dedicate it to those who represent the most important relationships in my life.

For the Past,

Firstly, I dedicate this book to the memory of those I have loved and lost:

To my dear grandparents, Arthur (1909-1993), Doris (1909-1988) and Winifred (1910-1983). And, most of all, to my beloved mother, Diana Tipper (1940-1985)

They left me with nothing I could spend, but everything I need.

Also to my beloved friend and companion, the 'D-Man' (1998-2005) who waited so patiently for me to come home every night and who left me in the middle of our last walk together, just as this book was being finalised.

For the Present,

As usual, I would also like to dedicate this book to Isabel, whose unflinching support has seen me through the best and the worst. Whether anyone will ever call me a 'great man' I do not know, but I do know that I have a great woman behind me.

Without her help, support and encouragement, this book, and the others I have written, could never have been.

For the Future,

Finally, I also dedicate this book to four very special young people: Michelle, Louise, James and Robert.

I can only hope that I will be able to leave them with all that they need.

C.B., Edinburgh, November 2005

Contents

Chapter 1

Introduction

1.1 TAX AND COUPLES

Most of us will be part of a couple for the majority of our adult lives. Generally speaking, this time also corresponds with our highest levels of both income and spending. Minimising our tax burden during this period is therefore absolutely essential.

Fortunately, the very fact that we are part of a couple also significantly expands our scope for personal tax planning. Between us, we have two personal allowances, two sets of tax bands and two 'bites of the cherry' when it comes to other key tax exemptions such as the annual Capital Gains Tax exemption and the nil rate band for Inheritance Tax.

But maximising the benefit of a couple's combined tax reliefs and exemptions is not always an easy matter and the way the tax legislation is structured and interpreted by Revenue & Customs will often be at odds with this objective.

We will therefore start out in Chapter 2 with an overview of tax planning for couples and by examining some of the tax planning strategies available to *all* couples, regardless of their tax status. Throughout this guide, however, it's essential to bear your own legal status in mind.

Chapter 2 contains lots of tax calculations, so please bear with me while we go through these as they lay the foundations for the chapters that follow. In fact, if you're not a 'numbers person' I would encourage you to read this chapter more than once to help all the information sink in!

In Chapter 3 we will deal with some of the more advanced planning techniques which are available to couples where one or both partners have their own business.

Having dealt with the tax planning strategies common to all couples, we then need to consider the fact that 'couples' operate within two very different tax regimes:

Firstly, there are 'unmarried couples', whose partnership has little or no legal status for tax purposes (nothing helpful, anyway). In the developed world of the early 21st Century, many couples now start their lives together with a period as an unmarried couple. Many will also choose to remain unmarried throughout their lives, especially since much of the former social stigma is now regarded as obsolete.

Until recently, same sex couples have had no choice but to remain unmarried. That situation changes with the Civil Partnership Act coming into force on 5th December 2005.

Nevertheless, since many people will spend at least part of their lives as an unmarried couple, Chapter 4 is devoted to examining the tax planning available specifically to unmarried couples.

Secondly, we have a different tax regime applying to married couples and, from 5th December 2005, registered civil partners.

Whilst, to the outside world, the couple may appear exactly the same as an unmarried couple, marriage or registered civil partnership makes an enormous difference to the couple's legal status, which includes their tax status.

The impact of this change is so great that one of my first questions to most new clients is "are you married?" (It never pays to make any assumptions on this matter, even if an octogenarian couple arrive in my office holding hands!) In future, of course, I may need to revise my question to "are you married or in a registered civil partnership?"

We will examine the legal and tax 'metamorphosis' brought about by marriage or registered civil partnership in detail in Chapters 5 and 6. The continuing ongoing tax planning available to married couples and registered civil partnerships is then covered in Chapter 7.

Another key change to a couple's tax status occurs if they separate or divorce. Like all of life's major changes, careful consideration can make a significant difference to the tax bills and we will look at this situation in Chapter 8.

Some of the issues specific to older couples are covered in Chapter 9 before we return, in Chapter 10, to a subject which ultimately affects all of us, Inheritance Tax.

Couples where one or both partners are non-UK resident or non-UK domiciled will be in a special position and we will examine their situation in Chapter 11. Readers who are in such a couple should therefore bear in mind that everything in the rest of this guide is subject to the further comments in Chapter 11.

Finally, whilst this is primarily a tax guide, in Chapter 12 we will take a brief look at some of the other legal and financial issues which couples need to take into account when planning their affairs.

Viewed as a whole, my objectives in writing this guide may be summarised as follows:

- To explore and explain the tax planning strategies available to *all* couples.
- To highlight the differences in tax treatment between married couples and registered civil partnerships on the one hand and unmarried couples on the other.
- To guide couples through the tax implications of the major changes to their tax status arising throughout their lives, whether brought about by marriage, civil partnership registration, divorce, separation or the death of a spouse or partner.

All in all, whether you've just met the love of your life or just celebrated your diamond wedding anniversary, I believe that there should be something for you in this guide.

1.2   WITH ALL MY WORLDLY GOODS

The traditional wedding vows used in many marriage ceremonies included the line "With All My Worldly Goods I Thee Endow". This implied a complete sharing of all wealth and possessions. The degree to which this implicit promise to share everything was actually adopted in practice always varied somewhat. Until fairly recently, UK tax law treated all of a married couple's possessions as belonging to the husband and a wife's status for tax purposes was that of a mere chattel!

Recent social and legal changes mean that we now operate in an environment where couples come in many different varieties and may also choose to share their wealth in many different ways.

Not everyone is comfortable with sharing wealth. Whatever their personal reasons may be, as a tax adviser I must always respect their wishes, whilst also advising them of the consequences.

One major consequence of an unwillingness to share your wealth with your partner is that this will hamper your ability to do constructive tax planning.

This springs from the fact that the most effective tax planning for couples usually requires the wealthier member of the couple to be willing to give some part of that wealth to the other partner. Some people are completely happy with this whilst, when it comes to money, others are very reluctant to trust their partners.

You must decide for yourself what level of 'sharing' you are comfortable with but I must stress that, as far as tax planning is concerned, the giving of any assets or income to your partner must be completely genuine in order to be effective. If you want to save tax, you are usually going to have to trust your partner. There are very few instances where you can 'have your cake and eat it'.

Those who are willing to consider what is most beneficial for the couple taken as a whole, and act accordingly, will usually have the greatest scope to utilise the available tax planning strategies.

Nevertheless, despite my line of work, I am always concerned to ensure that tax planning never takes precedence over common sense. After all, what would you rather do: give 40% of your money to Gordon Brown or allow an untrustworthy partner to run away with 100% of it?

1.3   SOME BASIC TERMINOLOGY

Before we proceed, it is probably worth me explaining a few basic tax principles and some of the terminology which I will be using in this guide.

The UK tax year runs from 6th April in one calendar year to 5th April in the next. Hence, the 2005/2006 tax year is the year ended 5th April 2006. Sometimes I will just refer to the tax year in this way, e.g. 2005/2006 or 2007/2008.

The UK comprises England, Scotland, Wales and Northern Ireland. For tax purposes, it does not include the Channel Islands or the Isle of Man.

Most readers will be familiar with the 'Inland Revenue' and many will also be aware of 'Customs & Excise'. On 18th April 2005, these two institutions were merged into a single body, 'Her Majesty's Revenue and Customs'.

The vast majority of the matters discussed in this guide would previously have concerned the Inland Revenue, as Customs & Excise dealt primarily with VAT and a few other indirect taxes.

Nevertheless, I have adopted the new name, 'Revenue & Customs', when referring to the tax authority in this guide.

A large part of this guide concerns the difference between couples who are legally married or in a registered civil partnership and couples who live together but are not in either of these formal legal institutions. (What we used to call 'living in sin', but I suspect that's a rather old-fashioned term now!)

Hence, it is very important for me to be quite precise with the terminology I use to describe our relationships. Therefore, in this guide, the following terms have only the exact meanings given below:

- **'Married'** means legally married and not separated or divorced.
- **'Husband'**, **'Wife'** and **'Spouse'** refer to spouses in a legal marriage only.
- **'Registered Civil Partner'** means a partner in a same sex couple who have legally registered their partnership and have not separated. I may also occasionally just refer to a **'civil partner'**.
- **'Registered Civil Partnership'** means a same sex couple who have legally registered their partnership and have not separated.
- **'Partner'** means any form of spouse or partner of the same or opposite sex with whom the taxpayer is co-habiting, or is otherwise in a long-term personal relationship. In this guide, this does not necessarily refer to a business partner – unless the taxpayer also happens to be co-habiting, or in a long-term personal relationship with the same person who happens to be their business partner also.
- **'Business partner'** is the term which I will use where I do specifically wish to refer to a person with whom the taxpayer is in business. Such a person may or may not also be the 'partner' with whom they have a personal relationship.
- **'Main Residence'** means the property which is regarded as your home, or principal private residence, for Capital Gains Tax purposes.

There are lots of tax calculations in this guide so it's also important to explain some of the more common tax calculation terminology. Current tax rates and allowances are listed in full in Appendix A.

Income Tax

- **Personal Allowance.** We all have a Personal Allowance which means the first £4,895 of income is tax free.

- **Starting Rate.** The next £2,090 of income is taxed at the 10% Starting Rate.

- **Basic Rate.** The next £30,310 of income is taxed at the Basic Rate, usually 22%.

- **Higher Rate.** Finally, any additional income is usually taxed at the 40% Higher Rate. If you add up the three numbers above you will see that once you earn more than **£37,295** you pay tax at the Higher Rate.

These tax rates do not all apply to all types of income, such as interest and dividends. For example, the Basic Rate for interest income is 20%. All this will be explained below.

There is also lots of mention of the term Tax Band. For example, the Basic Rate Tax Band is simply that £30,310 chunk of income which is taxed at the Basic Rate.

The above numbers will crop up many times in the examples that follow so it is definitely worth remembering them.

Capital Gains Tax

When it comes to Capital Gains Tax you will see frequent mention of the term Taper Relief. Generally speaking, the longer you hold an asset, such as property or shares, the more Taper Relief you qualify for.

For example, if you own a buy-to-let property for just over three years before selling it, you will qualify for 5% Taper Relief. In simplistic terms this means that 5% of your profits will be tax free. And if you hold onto the property for more than 10 years you will qualify for 40% Taper Relief – 40% of your profits will be tax free.

There are two different types of Taper Relief: Business Asset Taper Relief and Non-Business Asset Taper Relief. The latter is the most common and exempts between 5% and 40% of your profits, as described above.

Business Asset Taper Relief is far more generous and exempts 75% of your profits after just two years. Business assets include certain types of commercial property, most shares in private companies and most shares owned by company employees (see Appendix E for more information).

1.4   FUTURE TAX RATES & ALLOWANCES

In many of the examples throughout this guide, I will be considering the tax position of couples in *future* tax years.

Naturally, we don't know what the tax rates and allowances will be in future years.

What I have done, however, is adopt one consistent set of assumptions, based on past experience:

- Personal allowances will increase at the rate of 2.5% per year to compensate for inflation.

- All Income Tax and National Insurance rate bands will also increase at the same rate but the tax rates themselves will remain unchanged, except for a five pence per annum increase in the rate of Class 2 National Insurance Contributions.

- There will be no changes to the Corporation Tax regime.

The resultant future assumed tax rates are set out in Appendix B. Please do remember that these are simply for illustrative purposes and are only my 'best guess', so don't expect them to always be absolutely accurate.

1.5   OBTAINING TAX FORMS & INFORMATION

Any Revenue & Customs forms, leaflets, etc, referred to in this guide can be obtained from: www.hmrc.gov.uk or by calling into your local Tax Office.

There are also a number of telephone orderlines and I will try to give these where relevant.

In the absence of a specific phone number for the item you're looking for, the main Self Assessment orderline, 0845-9000-404, will probably be able to help.

1.6   SCOPE OF THIS GUIDE

The reader must bear in mind the general nature of this guide. Individual circumstances vary and all tax planning should be undertaken in the light of full knowledge of your individual circumstances.

Readers are advised to take professional advice before undertaking any tax planning – the author cannot take any responsibility for any actions taken by readers of this guide.

More specifically, I must also point out that this guide is concerned with planning a couple's UK taxation affairs only. I will, on a few occasions, have cause to mention foreign taxes but, in general, this guide is not concerned with foreign taxation. Whenever one or both of the couple have any form of foreign connection, foreign assets or foreign income, I would advise that local advice is sought in the relevant country.

One very important assumption which I have made throughout this guide is that we are concerned only with an adult couple, both of whom are aged 18 or more. Tax planning involving children under the age of 18 is a completely different matter and many of the techniques outlined herein simply will not work if you try to apply the same principles in a parent-child relationship or any other relationship which includes a person under the age of 18.

1.7   OTHER PEOPLE WISHING TO USE THIS GUIDE

Most of the tax planning available to unmarried couples will also be suitable for two adult siblings, a parent and their adult child, or any other pairs of adults wishing to arrange their tax affairs.

Some care still needs to be taken, however, as many of these 'pairs' will be connected persons (see section 5.8) and will therefore be subject to some of the same anti-avoidance legislation as a married couple. Furthermore, such people would not be regarded as 'co-habiting' which has important implications for tax credit claims (see section 2.19).

The best rule of thumb that I can offer any two adult people who are not a 'couple' but who still wish to plan their affairs to their mutual benefit is as follows:

- Check section 5.8 and Appendix C to see if you are connected.

- If not, you may plan your affairs on the same basis as an unmarried couple who are not co-habiting.

- If you are connected, you will probably suffer all of the same disadvantages as a married couple or registered civil partnership but without any of the advantages. If you proceed on this assumption, you probably won't go too far wrong but you will need to take professional advice to confirm your position.

Wealth Warning

What you must **not** do if you are connected is assume that you are in the same position as an unmarried couple.

Chapter 2

How Couples Save Tax

2.1 HOW DO COUPLES SAVE TAX?

In this chapter we are going to look at the general tax planning strategies available to **all couples**, regardless of whether they're married, unmarried or in a civil partnership.

I will concentrate on income and capital gains tax planning. Issues relating to the end of our time as a couple will be dealt with later in the book. The most significant of these is Inheritance Tax, which warrants a chapter of its own (Chapter 10).

Readers should bear in mind, however, that many of the 'lifetime' planning techniques discussed in the first few chapters of this book could also have Inheritance Tax consequences which will need to be considered.

How then, do couples save tax? The strategies which we use to save tax for a couple during their lifetime break down into three main categories:

- Sharing mutual wealth (known as Marginal Rate Planning),

- Controlling the timing of transactions, and

- Maximising the benefit of a partner's special tax status.

Throughout this chapter, we will look at each of these main tax planning categories for couples in turn. Many of the techniques which exploit the benefit of a partner's special tax status, however, relate to couples where one or both are non-UK resident or non-UK domiciled and will therefore be found in Chapter 11.

Couples where one or both partners are in business, whether as sole traders, partnerships or limited companies, are presented with a huge range of extra tax planning opportunities (and pitfalls!) and we will move on to these in Chapter 3.

2.2 SHARING MUTUAL WEALTH

Where a couple regard their wealth as entirely interchangeable and don't care which of them it belongs to, it is logical for them to plan their financial affairs to pay the least amount of tax.

Each member of the couple has their own set of tax allowances, reliefs, exemptions and rate bands, including:

- The personal Income Tax allowance
- The annual Capital Gains Tax exemption
- Private letting relief (for disposals of a current or former Principal Private Residence, i.e. your current or former home)
- The lower rate Income Tax band
- The basic rate Income Tax band
- The small earnings exception for Class 2 National Insurance
- The nil rate band for Inheritance Tax
- The annual exemption for Inheritance Tax
- The small gifts exemption for Inheritance Tax

The current amounts of each of these allowances, bands and reliefs applying for the 2005/2006 tax year are given in Appendix A, except for private letting relief, where the maximum relief per property per person is set at £40,000.

Every couple has the potential to double the value of these bands and reliefs – most of them on an *annual* basis.

2.3   HOW MUCH IS AT STAKE?

Let's consider for a moment how much the potential tax savings are actually worth in practice.

Using current 2005/2006 tax rates, the maximum tax savings available to most couples simply by optimising the use of their available reliefs are as follows:

- £3,400 in Capital Gains Tax **annually.**
  PLUS
- An extra £16,000 in Capital Gains Tax **per property** where private letting relief is available.
  PLUS
- A further £6,689 in Capital Gains Tax **annually,**
- £8,041 in Income Tax on rental income **annually,**
- £8,391 in Income Tax on UK dividend income **annually,**
- £8,432 in Income Tax and National Insurance Contributions on trading profits **annually,**
- £8,647 in Income Tax on savings income **annually,**
- £8,881 in Income Tax on foreign dividend income **annually, or**
- Some combination of the above.
  PLUS
- £110,000 in Inheritance Tax on death
  PLUS
- £1,200 **per annum** in Inheritance Tax on lifetime gifts
  PLUS
- A further £100 **per annum** in Inheritance Tax on small lifetime gifts **per recipient**
  PLUS
- A further £2,000 **per child** in Inheritance Tax on gifts made at the time of their marriage or registration of their civil partnership.

And this list is still not exhaustive!

Whilst simply making use of a person's tax allowances, exemptions and reliefs is not exactly considered to be 'rocket science' in the tax planning world, I would hope that the above list will have convinced most readers that it is nevertheless worthwhile.

Naturally to obtain the maximum benefit from sharing wealth, the couple does need to have a reasonable amount of wealth in the first place.

It currently takes combined annual income and capital gains of £74,590 before a couple are able to fully utilise their personal allowances and lower and basic rate tax bands.

Whilst all of the 'maximum savings' quoted in this chapter are based on the premise that the couple have this level of income between them, you will also see a great many examples of worthwhile savings being made by couples with much lower combined income levels.

In fact, *proportionally* the best savings come on the first slice of income which is 'shared' and a couple with a combined annual income of only £11,880 could conceivably save as much as £1,615 each year.

Just in case anyone does need convincing, however, I have prepared the following example of the lifetime tax savings that can be achieved by sharing wealth.

Lifetime Tax Savings Example

Two young brothers, Ollie and Stan, are each left substantial but identical legacies by their Great Aunt Mae. Each brother receives substantial interest income each year, over half of which is taxed at the 40% Higher Rate.

By 2005/2006 each brother is living with a long-term partner. Stan has transferred enough of his wealth to his partner Clara to enable her to fully utilise her personal allowance and her lower and basic rate

Income Tax bands. She also realises enough capital gains each year to make use of her own annual Capital Gains Tax exemption. Clara gave up her job when she moved in with Stan so she has no income other than that provided by the assets which Stan transferred to her.

Whilst Ollie supports his partner financially, he is not prepared to transfer any of his wealth and continues to keep all income and capital gains in his own name. Ollie's partner also gave up work a few years ago and is now quite happy to be supported by Ollie.

The only difference between Stan and Ollie at this stage is the fact that Stan has transferred wealth to Clara to enable her to utilise her own tax allowances, bands and reliefs. In 2005/2006 alone this saves the couple £12,047 in Income Tax and Capital Gains Tax. The money saved is all reinvested.

In 2006/2007, Stan and Clara make further tax savings of £13,128 by continuing to employ the same strategy, leaving them a total of £25,175 better off than Ollie and his partner after just two years. Again all the money saved is reinvested.

By 5th April 2015, simply by using Clara's personal allowance, Income Tax bands and annual Capital Gains Tax exemption for ten years, we find that she and Stan are a total of £178,108 better off than Ollie and his partner.

During 2014/2015, however, both couples also sold one of their former homes for a substantial capital gain. In each case, the gain on the property attracts private letting relief at the statutory maximum rate of £40,000 per person. Stan and Clara owned their property jointly and are thus entitled to a total of £80,000 private letting relief. Ollie, on the other hand, owned his property in his sole name and can claim only £40,000 in private letting relief. As a result of this, Stan and Clara save an additional £16,000 in Capital Gains Tax over and above the usual annual tax savings which they have already been enjoying.

Things carry on in the same vein for another ten years and, in 2024/2025, the couples both sell another former home under similar circumstances with the same overall additional tax saving accruing to Stan and Clara.

By this point we find that Stan and Clara are now £596,048 better off than Ollie.

In the years that follow, both couples undertake some Inheritance Tax planning by making use of the annual exemption for lifetime gifts of £3,000 per person. In each tax year Stan and Clara are able to make Inheritance Tax exempt gifts of £3,000 each, thus safely removing a total of £6,000 per annum from their estates for Inheritance Tax purposes. Ollie only uses his own annual Inheritance Tax exemption of £3,000 each year.

Between 6ᵗʰ April 2038 and 5ᵗʰ April 2045, each of Stan and Clara's four children marry or enter a registered civil partnership. On each occasion Stan and Clara are able to make additional Inheritance Tax exempt gifts of £5,000 each – a total of £10,000 on each occasion.

Each of Ollie's four children also marry or enter registered civil partnerships during the same period, but on each of these occasions, he only makes a single £5,000 Inheritance Tax exempt gift.

Tragically, on 6ᵗʰ April 2045, Stan, Clara, Ollie and Ollie's partner are all killed when a meteor hits their private space-yacht whilst in orbit around Mars. A few months later, the eight grieving cousins, the children of the two unlucky couples, gather in the offices of Grabbit & Runn, the family lawyers, to hear the details of their inheritance.

Firstly, Mr Grabbit the lawyer explains that Stan and Clara's accumulated Income Tax and Capital Gains Tax savings over a period of 40 years, together with the extra investment income which these reinvested savings have yielded mean that their estate is worth a total of £2,889,843 more than Ollie's estate.

He then further explains that Clara was able to make use of her own Inheritance Tax nil rate band, which over the years has risen to

£795,000. This, coupled with the Inheritance Tax exempt gifts made by Clara in the last seven years of her life means that a total of £836,000 extra has been sheltered from Inheritance Tax for the benefit of her and Stan's children.

All in all, after taking account of Inheritance Tax, Stan and Clara's children will eventually inherit £2,068,006 more than Ollie's children.

In the end, Stan's family is more than £2,000,000 better off simply because he was willing to share his wealth with his partner.

Well, it may have taken me 40 years, but I hope that I have now proved once and for all that this simple technique is as worthy as any complex tax planning scheme.

2.4   HOW AND WHY DOES SHARING MUTUAL WEALTH WORK?

The basic idea behind sharing mutual wealth is simply to move income or capital gains from the hands of one partner to the other.

Why does this save tax?

Moving income or capital gains saves tax when these are moved from a partner with a higher marginal tax rate to a partner with a lower marginal tax rate.

What do we mean by 'marginal tax rate'?

In simplistic terms, your marginal tax rate is the extra tax you pay on any increase in your income or capital gains. If you earn an extra £1 and your tax bill goes up by 30p, you have a 30% marginal tax rate.

Looked at another way, your marginal rate is the tax you can SAVE by transferring income or capital gains to your partner.

Matters get a bit more complex than this but let's kick off with a simple example.

Example

Ginger, a wealthy heiress, is in a long-term relationship with Fred, a freelance professional dancer whose income, shall we say, fluctuates.

In 2005/2006, Ginger's total income will be considerably in excess of the higher rate income tax threshold of £32,400.

Fred, on the other hand, expects total income for the year of only around £12,000. After deducting his personal allowance (£4,895), this leaves him with taxable income of just £7,105, some £27,505 less than the higher rate threshold.

In April 2005, Ginger transfers a bank deposit of £500,000 into Fred's name. During 2005/2006 this deposit will yield interest income of £25,000. As Fred is a basic rate taxpayer, his Income Tax liability on this interest income will only be £5,000 (20%).

If Ginger had kept the bank deposit in her own name, she would have had an Income Tax liability of £10,000 on this income (i.e. 40%).

In this example, we can easily see that one very simple transaction has saved the couple £5,000 tax in one year alone.

This makes perfect sense when you view the couple's wealth as being completely interchangeable.

On the other hand, one might wonder just who this 'Fred' really is. In addition to the £5,000 tax saving, he now also has a further £515,000 which would otherwise have belonged to Ginger. This type of planning therefore involves a great deal of trust!

19

So far we have seen why it is that couples are able to save tax by sharing mutual wealth and just how much is at stake. But exactly how is this done?

Much of the tax planning associated with sharing mutual wealth will involve transferring assets to your partner. The tax consequences of the actual transfer of assets will depend on the couple's *marital status*. We will have to return to this in later chapters.

For the time being we will ignore the tax consequences of the actual transfer of any assets and concentrate just on the subsequent tax savings that can be enjoyed.

Before we do that, however, I need to further explain the marginal tax rate concept.

2.5   USING MARGINAL RATES TO SAVE TAX

In the previous section, I used the expression 'marginal rate of tax'. This refers to the rate of tax which the taxpayer suffers on any increase in income or capital gains.

The concept of a 'marginal rate of tax' is absolutely vital in tax planning since it also governs the rate at which we are able to save tax by reducing a person's income or capital gains.

In the case of a couple, our ability to save tax through sharing mutual wealth is therefore based on the difference between one partner's marginal rate and another partner's marginal rate.

We saw a simple example of this principle in the previous section. Ginger's marginal rate of tax on interest income was 40%, but Fred's was only 20%. By moving income from Ginger to Fred we were therefore able to save tax at the rate of 20%.

Sadly, it isn't always that simple!

To fully understand the marginal tax rate concept, you have to understand that your annual income is treated as if it were composed of *layers*.

Different tax rates apply to the different layers.

Our layers of income are arranged as follows:

- At the bottom, we have our employment or self-employment income.

- Next comes any income from land and property (usually rental income).

- On top of these goes our interest income and any other investment income not classed as a dividend.

- Finally, at the top of our income, go any dividends we receive.

If we have any capital gains, they go right at the very top, on top of all of our income for the year.

As a result of this layer system, employment and self-employment income get first call on our personal allowances and lower tax rates. The benefit of this, however, is offset somewhat by the fact that we must also pay National Insurance on this income.

As far as I'm concerned, National Insurance Contributions are simply additional tax and, hence, when undertaking any tax planning, we must treat them as tax. This can lead to some strange quirks in taxpayers' marginal tax rates, as we shall soon see.

Furthermore, when considering couples, one of the partners in the couple may also be the other partner's employer. This brings employer's secondary National Insurance Contributions into play as an additional factor which must also be considered in any tax planning which we undertake.

The 'Layer System' Of Taxing Income & Gains

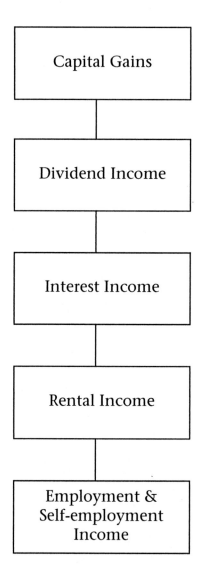

The important point for couples doing tax planning is that the different types of income (or layers) are taxed at different rates.

In the next few pages I'm going to briefly explain how salaries, business profits, rents, interest and dividends are all taxed before showing you the maximum tax savings that can be achieved by transferring each of these types of income to your partner.

For men aged under 65 and women aged under 60 at the end of the tax year, the combined rates of Income Tax and National Insurance Contributions on their 2005/2006 employment or self-employment income may be summarised as follows:

Employment & Self-Employment Income 2005/2006
Combined Income Tax and National Insurance Rates

		Employment	Self-Employment	Employer NI
First	£4,895	0%	0%	0%
£4,895 - £6,985		10%+**11%**= 21%	10%+**8%**= 18%	**12.8%**
£6,985 - £32,760		22%+**11%**= 33%	22%+**8%**= 30%	**12.8%**
£32,760 - £37,295		22%+**1%**= 23%	22%+**1%**= 23%	**12.8%**
Over	£37,295	40%+**1%**= 41%	40%+**1%**= 41%	**12.8%**

The bold numbers are national insurance rates. The other numbers are the more familiar income tax rates.

Other forms of income are not subject to National Insurance.

However, they will be forced up into higher rates of tax by the layer system.

When considering investment income it is therefore important to remember that any of the low-tax bands already used up by your employment or self-employment income will not be available.

Subject to the above comments, the Income Tax rates applying to other income received during 2005/2006 by taxpayers aged under 65 at the end of the tax year may be summarised as follows:

Investment Income (Rent, Interest, Dividends) 2005/2006
Income Tax Rates

		Rents	Interest	UK Dividends	Foreign Dividends
First		£4,895	0%	0%	0%	0%
£4,895	-	£6,985	10%	10%	0%	10%
£6,985	-	£37,295	22%	20%	0%	10%
Over		£37,295	40%	40%	25%	32.5%

So if you have £4,895 of interest income and no other income you will pay no tax. If you also have, say, a £60,000 salary, thanks to the layer system your interest income will be forced up into the 40% tax band.

Lastly, we must consider capital gains. These form the top layer and will therefore be the last to benefit from a taxpayer's lower rate and basic rate tax bands.

Furthermore, the tax-free personal allowance is not available at all for capital gains.

In place of the personal allowance each taxpayer has an annual Capital Gains Tax exemption which protects £8,500 of capital gains from the taxman.

Capital Gains Tax is an extremely complex subject in its own right and there are lots of reliefs which you can claim. For the moment, however, the following table sets out the rate of Capital Gains Tax applying to a taxpayer's *taxable* capital gains for 2005/2006:

Taxable Capital Gains 2005/2006
Capital Gains Tax Rates

		Capital Gains	
First	£8,500	0%	
£8,500 -	£10,590	10%	Where lower rate band still available
£10,590 -	£40,900	20%	Where basic rate band still available
Over	£40,900	40%	

Notes To Tax Rate Tables

i)   The equivalent tables for women aged 60 or more and men aged 65 or more are shown in section 9.7.

ii) 'Self-employment' income in the first table above includes trading partnerships. Those with £4,345 or more must also pay Class 2 National Insurance of £2.10 per week.

iii) Where a taxpayer has both employment and self-employment income in the same tax year a statutory maximum limit of national insurance will apply instead.

iv) The rates shown above for UK dividends are the effective rates payable on the actual cash dividend received. The actual calculation is somewhat more complex and is set out in section 2.12.

To understand the way the layer system works and how to interpret the above tables we need to look at an example. This example is also a useful illustration of how your tax bill is calculated if you have income from many sources.

We'll then take the example a step further to explain the marginal rate concept and why it is so important for couples doing constructive tax planning.

Example

During the tax year 2005/2006, Buster receives employment income of £10,000, rental income of £20,000, interest income of £15,000, UK dividends of £1,000 and a taxable capital gain of £10,000.

Buster's total tax bill for the year is calculated as follows:

	£
Employment Income - £10,000	
£10,000 less £4,895 Personal allowance	
leaves £5,105 taxable:	
Income Tax @ 10% on £2,090	209.00
Income Tax @ 22% on remaining £3,015	663.30
National Insurance @ 11% on £5,105	561.55
Rental Income - £20,000	
Income Tax @ 22%	4,400.00
Interest Income - £15,000	
Income Tax @ 20% on remaining basic rate	
tax band (£37,295 - £10,000 - £20,000 = £7,295)	1,459.00
Income Tax @ 40% on remaining £7,705	3,082.00
Dividend Income - £1,000	
Income Tax @ 25% on UK Dividends	250.00
Taxable Capital Gains - £10,000	
£10,000 less £8,500 Annual Exemption	
Leaves £1,500 taxable	
Capital Gains Tax @ 40%	600.00
Total Tax Liability for the year:	**11,224.85**

You'll notice that Buster's interest income eventually pushes him into the 40% tax band. He becomes a Higher Rate taxpayer when his income passes £37,295. But what is Buster's marginal tax rate – is it 40% perhaps? Well, maybe, yes, but actually he doesn't have one marginal rate of tax but *four different ones!*

Example Part 2

The facts are exactly the same as above, except that Buster's rental income goes up by £1,000 to £21,000. The tax calculation again:

	£
Employment Income - £10,000	
£10,000 less £4,895 Personal allowance	
leaves £5,105 taxable:	
Income Tax @ 10% on £2,090	209.00
Income Tax @ 22% on remaining £3,015	663.30
National Insurance @ 11% on £5,105	561.55
Rental Income - £21,000	
Income Tax @ 22%	4,620.00
Interest Income - £15,000	
Income Tax @ 20% on remaining basic rate	
tax band (£37,295 - £10,000 - £21,000 = £6,295)	1,259.00
Income Tax @ 40% on remaining £8,705	3,482.00
Dividend Income - £1,000	
Income Tax @ 25% on UK Dividends	250.00
Taxable Capital Gains - £10,000	
£10,000 less £8,500 Annual Exemption	
Leaves £1,500 taxable	
Capital Gains Tax @ 40%	600.00
Total Tax Liability for the year:	**11,644.85**

An extra £1,000 of income has increased Buster's tax bill by £420 – a marginal tax rate of 42%. This means that if he can transfer this income to a partner who doesn't pay tax he could save £420.

How did we get 42% - a rate that doesn't even appear in any of the tables?

The 42% rate is simply a product of the layer system. This rate is made up of the 22% tax payable on the extra rental income plus an *extra* 20% payable on some of Buster's interest income.

The extra £1,000 of rental income pushed an additional £1,000 of Buster's interest income up out of the 20% tax band and into the 40% tax band, hence costing him an extra 20% in tax.

Similarly if Buster earned an extra £1,000 of employment income he would pay an extra £530 in tax – a marginal tax rate of 53%!

This is made up of Income Tax on that income at 22%, National Insurance on it at 11% and an extra 20% on £1,000 of interest income pushed into the 40% tax band.

Buster's other marginal rates can be derived more easily and are:

- 40%, which he would pay on any extra interest income or capital gains, and

- 25%, which he would pay on any extra UK dividends received.

Where Does This Leave Tax Planning For Couples?

It is the difference between a couple's marginal tax rates *on the same income* which lets them save tax by moving income or capital gains between them.

What we can now see is that establishing your marginal tax rate is not as easy as it may at first seem. Your marginal tax rate depends not only on your overall position but also on which *type* of income we are looking at.

Nevertheless, the principle remains that a couple will save tax whenever they are able to move income or capital gains from the partner with the higher marginal rate to the partner with the lower marginal rate.

The difference between these two rates, the 'marginal rate differential', is the rate at which we are able to save tax.

For Ginger and Fred, the marginal rate differential was 20%. This rate applied to £25,000 of income which was moved and thus resulted in a tax saving of £5,000.

Going back to the £2,000,000 tax saving of Stan and Clara (section 2.3), their first year's tax saving of £12,047 can now be explained as follows:

Example Revisited

Stan was so wealthy that his marginal tax rate was 40% on his interest income and his capital gains.

Clara had no other income of her own so the marginal rate differential on the first £4,895 of interest income transferred to her was 40%.

You calculate this by taking Stan's marginal rate of 40% and subtracting Clara's marginal rate of 0% on her tax-free personal allowance]. This therefore saved £1,958 in Income Tax.

The marginal rate differential on the next £2,090 of income was 30% [Stan's 40% less Clara's 10% Lower Rate] and this saved another £627.

The next £30,310 of transferred income had a marginal rate differential of 20% [Stan's 40% less Clara's 20%] and further reduced the couple's combined Income Tax bill by a total of £6,062.

This all added up to a total Income Tax saving of £8,647.

On top of this, the couple were also able to move capital gains of £8,500 from Stan's marginal rate of 40% to Clara's 0% by using her annual Capital Gains Tax exemption.

This saved a further £3,400, bringing the couple's total tax saving for 2005/2006 to £12,047.

2.6 WHY IS MARGINAL RATE TAX PLANNING SO IMPORTANT FOR COUPLES?

If couples were like identical twins, where everything was exactly the same for each of them, then there would be no scope for marginal rate tax planning.

This is because this form of tax planning, and indeed the whole strategy of sharing mutual wealth, depends on exploiting the differences in the couple's tax positions.

But don't despair if you and your partner find that you are unable to identify any marginal rate differentials to exploit.

What this will usually mean is that you have already shared your mutual wealth quite successfully and are probably making optimum use of your combined tax reliefs and exemptions without the need for any further action.

Probably!

In practice though, I find that most couples do have some scope to benefit from some marginal rate tax planning.

There are a number of reasons for this:

- Firstly, there is the complexity of the tax system itself, which throws up so many different marginal rates of tax. (Remember Buster and his four different marginal rates?)

- Secondly, when it comes to Capital Gains Tax, most people will start with an effective marginal rate of 0% on their first £8,500 of capital gains – their annual exemption. This then, tends to be one of our most fruitful areas for marginal rate tax planning.

- Thirdly, we will often find that one partner will have set up a business while the other may, at least initially, remain in employment. This inevitably creates marginal rate differentials for us to exploit.

- And lastly, there are social reasons. Often one partner will be responsible for the care of the couple's children and, for some period at least, may have no income of their own without the benefit of some marginal rate planning.

Take all these factors together and we find that marginal rate planning is a powerful tool in tax planning for couples.

2.7 MARGINAL RATE TAX PLANNING FOR COUPLES: A SIMPLE GUIDE

Following the complexities of some of the previous sections, I thought it might be useful here if I provided a simple 6 Step guide to marginal rate tax planning for couples:

Step 1
Identify any income or capital gains which it may be possible to move from one partner to the other and where such a move would result in a tax saving.

Step 2

Calculate each partner's marginal rate of tax on each type of income or capital gains identified under Step 1.

Step 3

Calculate the marginal rate differential for each type of income or capital gains.

Step 4

Identify the income or gain with the highest marginal rate differential.

Step 5

Move as much of that income or gain as you can until you reach the point where one of the partners' marginal rate of tax on that income changes.

Step 6

Repeat Steps 1 to 5 until you are no longer able to identify any income or gains under Step 1.

An Even Simpler Method?

If you can, why not just share everything equally?

In many cases this produces the best tax result and, if you can't be bothered with all of the messy calculations involved in following my 6 Step guide, it's probably as good a rule of thumb as you're going to get.

It's not foolproof though, as we shall see later.

By now, you should have a good idea how to carry out steps 2 to 4 of my 6-step guide above but we haven't really dealt with the mechanics of how to carry out steps 1 and 5. This is because these steps depend very much on what type of income or gains you are dealing with.

We will therefore now move on in the following sections to the mechanics of 'moving income and gains' of various different types.

2.8   WHAT DOES MOVING INCOME OR CAPITAL GAINS MEAN?

In previous sections I have referred to the idea of 'moving' income or capital gains. This may have been slightly misleading since it is not possible to move just the income or the capital gain.

In every case, there will need to be some form of structural change which will provide the partner with the income or capital gain.

Much of this planning will involve moving the *underlying assets* which provide the income or capital gain. That transfer in itself will generally have its own tax consequences – typically Capital Gains Tax, Inheritance Tax or both. These consequences, however, depend on the couple's marital status and will therefore need to be covered in later chapters.

In this chapter I will simply point out what needs to be done and point you in the direction of the chapter which deals with the consequences.

In addition to the potential tax consequences, the reader must also beware that a transfer of assets to a partner must be absolutely genuine in order to be effective for tax purposes.

Those assets will be your partner's to deal with as they wish. They will keep them if you separate and they may not deal with them quite as you might have expected in their will either.

2.9   HOW TO MOVE INCOME & GAINS SUCCESSFULLY

The reason I am inclined to stress the point about *genuine* transfers so much is the fact that so many attempts to save tax by sharing a couple's mutual wealth have come to grief in the courts because the wealthier member of the couple has tried to keep control of the money and has not genuinely given it to the partner.

Before I explain how you can move income and gains successfully, here is an example of how <u>not</u> to do it:

Example

Michael, a very wealthy man, marries Catherine, a young actress.

On the eve of their wedding, acting on his lawyer's advice, Michael gets Catherine to sign a pre-nuptial agreement to the effect that anything that he gives to her during the course of their marriage must be returned to him in the event that they separate or divorce.

A couple of years later Michael gives Catherine part of his investment property portfolio. The documentation drawn up at the time of this gift includes the clause 'subject to pre-nuptial agreement'.

A little while later, Michael is enjoying a drink after a round of golf with his father and is boasting how he is saving over £8,000 a year in Income Tax by having put some of his investment properties into Catherine's name.

"Gee son", responds his father, "I'm not sure if that is such a good idea. Are you sure you can trust her? She's been getting awfully friendly with that young tennis pro lately. You know the one, Antonio, I think his name is."

"Don't sweat pop", replies Michael. "I've got it covered."

Unfortunately for Michael, his conversation with his father is overheard by Antonio.

Antonio is an ambitious young man and no fool either. He writes an anonymous letter to Revenue & Customs relaying the contents of Michael and his father's conversation.

Revenue & Customs launch an investigation into Michael's tax affairs which uncovers the pre-nuptial agreement. They conclude that the transfer of properties to Catherine is nothing but a sham and promptly assess Michael for the £8,000 or so a year in Income Tax which he had supposedly saved by moving a large part of his rental income to Catherine.

Settlements

The reason that Michael's tax planning failed is something called the 'settlements legislation'.

A 'settlement' in tax terminology is basically a gift. If you give your partner £1,000, you have 'settled' £1,000 on them. You would then be referred to as the 'settlor' and your partner would be the beneficiary of this 'settlement'.

The settlements legislation states that the settlor will continue to pay tax on income or capital gains arising from the asset if he or she still has an interest in the assets.

Example

Bill gives Ben some shares. This is a settlement. Bill is the settlor. The shares are the settled assets.

Before giving the shares to Ben, Bill gets Ben to sign an agreement stating that the shares must be returned to Bill if he so requests.

This means that Bill has retained an interest in the shares.

Bill will therefore continue to be taxed on the income (dividends) and might also be liable for Capital Gains Tax if the shares are sold, depending on the exact terms of his agreement with Ben.

Wealth Warning

Retaining rights over any assets or funds which you transfer to your partner will result in the relevant income or gains continuing to be taxed in your hands.

Tax Tip

Jointly held assets, however, provide something of an exception to this general rule. As one of the joint owners, you will naturally retain some rights over the underlying assets. This is a special case, which we will examine further in the next section.

Leaving jointly held assets to one side for the moment, the general rule is that, in order to 'move' income or gains to your partner successfully, you must ensure that you do not retain any rights over the underlying assets.

In addition to legal rights, it is also wise to ensure that you do not actually receive the relevant income or sale proceeds.

I therefore recommend the following measures whenever transferring assets or funds to a partner for tax planning purposes:

1. Do not retain any continuing interest in the assets.

The transferred assets or funds must be theirs to do with as they wish. If you think this is too risky then you may have to accept that saving tax is not truly your top priority. A few alternatives do exist, as we shall see later.

2. Make sure any legal documentation is done properly.

You must make sure that the transfer has full legal effect. This means preparing formal transfer documentation in the same way that it would be done for a transfer to a third party (e.g. a conveyance on transfer of land and buildings). Don't skimp on this.

3. Register the transfer with the appropriate authorities.

Some types of transfer do not have full legal effect until they are registered with the appropriate authorities. Transfers of land and property need to be registered with the Land Registry; share transfers must be notified to the relevant Company Secretary and subsequently notified to Companies House on the company's next Annual Return. (We will deal with share issues in the next Chapter.)

4. Make sure you do not receive any income or sale proceeds.

Many people make the mistake of transferring assets to their partner but then allowing the income to continue to be paid into their own bank account or into a joint bank account. There are some potential ways around this problem but the simplest and safest solution is to ensure that future income is paid direct to your partner and that they pay it into a bank account in their sole name.

The same goes for any sale proceeds from a transferred asset when we are looking at 'moving' capital gains.

5. Make sure that your partner knows what you are doing.

Amazingly enough, many a partner has found out that they have technically been 'enjoying' some income for many years which they knew nothing about. Apart from the inevitable problems which this causes in the divorce courts (which is where this sort of thing often 'comes out in the wash'), this can provide Revenue & Customs with sufficient grounds to invoke the settlements legislation and tax the transferor partner on all of the income.

I would suggest that your partner is not truly 'receiving' income or sale proceeds if they don't actually know about it. It is important to make sure that they are kept advised of any transfers.

6. Make sure that any payments are clearly made.

If the transferee is to pay the transferor for the asset, this payment should go into an account in the transferor partner's sole name only. Actual payment in cash should be made whenever possible. If sums are merely left outstanding as a 'loan' there is always a danger of Revenue & Customs arguing that the transaction was never completed.

Naturally, following some of the above recommendations will have a financial cost. If that cost outweighs your potential tax savings, the answer is **not** to try to push it through 'on the cheap'. This would be a waste of time as your tax planning measures would probably fail. The correct answer is to find another way to do your tax planning.

Before carrying out any transfer you also need to consider any actual or potential tax costs involved. I have already mentioned Capital Gains Tax and Inheritance Tax and we will be covering these in later chapters. You may also need to consider Stamp Duty or Stamp Duty Land Tax, which we shall look at in section 2.24 and, in a few instances, VAT, which is covered in section 3.12.

The settlements legislation applies to all couples regardless of their marital status.

Indeed, it applies to all transfers of assets or funds from one person to another. The recommendations set out above are therefore equally important for all couples.

An additional quirk of the legislation, however, is that it may also be invoked whenever the settlor's spouse retains an interest in the transferred assets. At first glance, this might seem to suggest that any attempt to move income or gains between married people or civil partners is doomed to failure. Thankfully, there are some important exemptions which prevent this from being the case. Nevertheless, this aspect of the legislation does create further difficulties for married couples and registered civil partnerships which we shall return to in subsequent chapters.

Tax Tip

Just before we leave this subject, I would, at this point, like to point out that Michael in our example was particularly badly advised, as rental income is one type of income where there *is* in fact great scope to retain control over much of the capital value in your property and still make use of your partner's lower tax rates.

We will therefore return to this subject in sections 4.9 and 7.5.

2.10   JOINTLY HELD ASSETS

Holding assets jointly often provides scope to move income or capital gains, while still retaining some control over the underlying assets.

Recent changes in tax law have diminished the benefits of joint ownership a little in the case of married couples and we will be looking at their position later, in Chapter 7.

For the moment though, let's just look at some of the basic principles of joint ownership and how it affects a couple's tax planning.

Joint Bank Accounts

These remain a perfectly viable and very simple way of sharing wealth with your partner.

Generally speaking, the interest income on a joint account will be treated as accruing equally to both partners and will be taxed 50:50. Revenue & Customs would expect this treatment to be followed in the vast majority of cases.

It might be possible for a couple to alter this income split, perhaps by way of a deed but in practice the danger of Revenue & Customs enforcing an equal split is so great that the couple would be far better to simply restructure their finances and use separate accounts.

If restrictions are placed on one partner's access to the account and Revenue & Customs believes that this creates a tax advantage, then they could apply the settlements legislation and tax the unrestricted partner on all the income.

So if you try to use a joint account to do anything other than share both the capital and interest income equally, it's really a case of 'Heads The Taxman Wins, Tails You Lose'.

As I explained in the previous section, it is sensible to ensure that income or sales proceeds from any transferred assets are not paid into a joint account.

Furthermore, if you are trying to make a gift or a cash payment to your partner, it may not be sufficiently clear that the gift or payment has been made if the funds are deposited in a joint account.

Income from other jointly held assets which <u>is</u> to be split equally, can be safely paid into a joint account. To be on the safe side, however, the division of income is always far clearer if it is paid into accounts in each partner's sole name whenever possible.

Furthermore, if the income from the other joint assets is <u>not</u> to be split equally, it is really sensible to ensure that it is not paid into a joint account, as this would generally imply an equal split of the income.

Jointly Held Property – Land and Buildings

After the joint bank account, the next most common form of jointly held property in the UK is land and buildings, sometimes referred to as 'real property'.

In England and Wales, there are two different legal forms for jointly held real property:

- Joint Tenants or
- Tenants in Common

In Scotland, joint ownership of property comes in only one form called 'Pro Indivisio' ownership and this is the same as Tenants in Common.

Joint Tenants

With joint tenants the ownership of each person's share passes automatically on death to the other person. This is known as 'survivorship'. Furthermore, neither joint owner is normally able to sell their share of the property without the consent of the other.

The capital gain on the disposal of a property held as joint tenants will always be split equally.

This severely restricts the scope for Capital Gains Tax planning. It is also often quite disadvantageous for Inheritance Tax purposes.

Joint tenancies are therefore generally less desirable than Tenancies in Common from a tax planning perspective.

Having said that, the security provided by the right of 'survivorship' will often be of more value to many couples.

Tenants in Common

Pro Indivisio ownership in Scotland and Tenancies in Common in England and Wales both operate in much the same way as each other.

The joint owners are each free to do as they wish with their own share of the property and there is no right of survivorship.

The joint owners' shares in the property need not be equal. This opens up an almost infinite range of possibilities for Capital Gains Tax planning when the property is sold.

Without this more flexible joint ownership we would have only three choices:

- One partner holds the whole property,
- The other partner holds the whole property, or
- Both partners hold the property equally.

Under Pro Indivisio ownership or a Tenancy in Common we can consider many other possibilities.

Example

John and Lee plan to invest £3,000,000 in a new commercial property development which will be rented out to Tesda plc, a large national supermarket chain.

They plan to sell the property in two years' time and anticipate making a capital gain of £1,000,000.

Because John also works part-time for Tesda as a non-executive director, he will be entitled to 75% Business Asset Taper relief – this essentially means he only has to pay tax on 25% of his profits. This means John will only pay tax at 10% on his capital gain (40% x 25% = 10%).

If John owned the whole property the Capital Gains Tax bill would be £100,000.

John's partner Lee has also dabbled in property investment in the past. Sadly, however, he was not too successful and has brought forward capital losses of £190,900. That was some years ago, however, and Lee is also now a higher rate taxpayer.

The sale is anticipated to take place during 2007/2008, when the Capital Gains Tax annual exemption is expected to be £9,100. John, however, expects to have several other capital gains in 2007/2008 which will therefore use up his annual exemption. Lee's 2007/2008 annual exemption, on the other hand, will probably be available to use against the gain on the supermarket investment.

John and Lee see the new investment as an opportunity to utilise Lee's losses and annual exemption. However, as Lee does not work for Tesda plc, any net gain over and above the total of his brought forward losses and annual exemption would be taxed at 40%.

If John and Lee were to own the property jointly in equal shares, their Capital Gains Tax liabilities on the sale would be as follows:

	John	**Lee**
Sale Proceeds	£2,000,000	£2,000,000
Less: Cost	£1,500,000	£1,500,000
	---------------	---------------
Capital Gain	£500,000	£500,000
Less:		
Losses brought forward:	-	£190,900
	---------------	---------------
	£500,000	£309,100
Taper Relief @ 75% (John only)	£375,000	-
	---------------	---------------
	£125,000	£309,100
Annual Exemption (Lee only)	-	£9,100
	---------------	---------------
Taxable Gains	£125,000	£300,000
	=========	=========
Capital Gains Tax @ 40%:	£50,000	£120,000

The couple's total tax bill would thus be £170,000, which, quite disastrously, is £70,000 **more** than if John had simply held the property in his sole name.

Which is where a Tenancy in Common comes in handy (or buying your property in Scotland). As tenants in common, John and Lee are able to divide their interest in the property in the proportion 80/20 instead of 50/50. Using this form of joint ownership, their Capital Gains Tax liabilities on the sale of the property in 2007/2008 may now be computed as follows:

	John	*Lee*
Sale Proceeds	£3,200,000	£800,000
Less:		
Cost	£2,400,000	£600,000
Capital Gain	£800,000	£200,000
Less:		
Losses brought forward:	-	£190,900
	£800,000	£9,100
Taper Relief @ 75% (John only)	£600,000	-
	£200,000	£9,100
Annual Exemption (Lee only)	-	£9,100
Taxable Gains	£200,000	Nil
Capital Gains Tax @ 40%:	£80,000	Nil

The couple's total tax bill would thus be £80,000. Not only is this considerably better than that which would have arisen under equal joint ownership, but they have also saved £20,000 compared to the position where the property was held by John alone.

Income From Jointly Held Real Property

The scope for planning in relation to income from jointly held real property is dependent on the couple's marital status, so we shall return to this subject in later chapters.

Putting Assets Into Joint Names

A couple will often be able to achieve tax savings by transferring assets into joint names, rather than transferring the whole asset from one partner to the other.

Where the asset was originally owned by one person only, in order to satisfy the settlements legislation, it's vital that the person making the transfer does not retain any rights over the other person's share of the assets.

If, for example, one partner owns a house outright and agrees to put it into joint names on condition that the whole house will return to them if they separate, this would be an additional right over and above the normal rights of joint ownership.

This would mean that, in the event that the property was ever rented out, the settlements legislation could be applied to tax all of the rental income on the partner who made the transfer.

Whilst I have never seen the point taken in practice, this also suggests that it would be unwise to transfer a property from your sole name into a *joint tenancy* with your partner when you are making the transfer for tax planning purposes.

Tax Tip

It will generally be wise to use a Tenancy in Common when transferring property into joint ownership with your partner.

Finally, when putting assets into joint ownership with your partner, I would repeat my recommendations from the previous section, adapted slightly, as follows:

1. Do not retain any interest in your partner's share.

2. Make sure any legal documentation is done properly.

3. Register joint ownership with appropriate authorities.

4. Do not receive your partner's share of any income.

5. Make sure your partner knows what you're doing.

6. Make sure payments are clearly made.

2.11   INTEREST INCOME

Generally speaking, interest income is the easiest type of taxable income to get into your partner's hands. This is probably the simplest, most basic, piece of tax planning any couple can do.

In fact, this was actually the first piece of tax planning which I was ever able to do for myself.

Some years ago, I was in a well-paid job with a large accountancy firm and was thus a higher rate taxpayer. My then wife was looking after our young children and hence had no taxable income of her own.

We had a few modest savings in joint deposit accounts. The drawback to this, of course, was the fact that I had to pay 40% Income Tax on my share of the interest we received.

As soon as the advent of 'separate taxation' (see section 7.1) arrived, I transferred all of our savings into accounts in my wife's sole name. Our modest interest income was all covered by her personal allowance and hence we saved tax at 40%.

Of course, when we subsequently divorced, she kept all of the savings. In other words, I saved 40% of the income but lost 100% of the capital!

Ah well, we live and learn. It certainly helps to have such an experience behind me when advising clients on the benefits of common sense over tax planning.

Nevertheless, the tax planning at the heart of my actions was perfectly sound and all a couple needs to do to save tax on their interest income is to transfer the necessary funds into the sole name of the partner with the lower marginal tax rate.

The *maximum* possible annual tax savings that can be generated by moving interest income from a higher rate taxpayer to a partner with no other income are made up as follows:

£4,895	@	40%	(	40%	-	0%	)	=	£1,958.00
£2,090	@	30%	(	40%	-	10%	)	=	£627.00
£30,310	@	20%	(	40%	-	20%	)	=	£6,062.00
							Total		£8,647.00

What's happening in this case is the poorer partner's tax-free allowance, 10% tax band and 20% tax band are all used up by transferring income.

The other good news here is that, if you don't have enough interest income to achieve the full saving shown above, it is the first amount transferred which achieves the biggest saving.

For example, a transfer of just £1,000 of interest income from a higher rate taxpayer to a partner with no other income will save Income Tax at 40% - i.e. £400.

One downside to such a transfer is there may be Inheritance Tax consequences when the transferor dies within seven years of the transfer. See Chapter 10 for more details.

UK banks and building societies are generally required to deduct Income Tax at 20% from payments of interest to all UK resident taxpayers.

Hence, if interest income is received by a partner with little or no other income it will usually be necessary to make a tax reclaim. This can be done by completing form R40 which should then be submitted to Revenue & Customs.

Two possible alternatives are as follows:

- The low income partner could deposit their funds abroad and receive interest gross. If their total income exceeds the £4,895 personal allowance they will then need to complete a Tax Return and pay over any tax which is due.

- If the partner's total income is not expected to exceed the personal allowance, they may claim to have their UK bank interest paid gross. This can be done by completing form R85. This form should be handed in to your bank, **not** the Tax Office.

   In the event that their total income does end up exceeding the personal allowance, they will again need to complete a Tax Return and pay over any tax which is due.

Forms R40 and R85 can be obtained from the 'Taxback' orderline: 0845-0776-543 or by faxing a request to: 0845-9000-604.

Readers may also find it useful to order Revenue & Customs leaflet IR111 which provides guidance on how and when to complete form R85.

2.12   UK DIVIDEND INCOME

In section 2.5, I set out two rates of tax for UK dividend income: 25% for higher-rate taxpayers and 0% for everyone else.

These are the effective tax rates on the actual amount of dividend you receive and most of the time are the only rates you need to think about.

The true position is slightly more complicated and sometimes when we are doing marginal rate tax planning we need to be aware of the full mechanics of how UK dividends are taxed.

So please bear with me while we go through the calculations!

When a UK dividend (a dividend from a UK company) is paid, it is treated as having a tax credit attached to it. The amount of the tax credit is equal to one ninth of the amount of dividend actually paid. For tax purposes, the total or 'gross' dividend is the actual or 'net' dividend paid plus the one ninth tax credit.

Example

Dividend paid:	*£900*
Tax Credit (1/9):	*£100*
Gross dividend (10/9ths):	*£1,000*

The true tax rates applied to the *gross dividend* are then 32.5% for higher rate taxpayers and 10% for everyone else. A deduction is then allowed for the tax credit attached to the dividend.

Example

Rachel and Ross each receive a UK dividend of £900.

Rachel is currently working as a waitress and is a basic rate taxpayer. The tax on her dividend is therefore calculated as follows:

Dividend received:	*£900*
Plus tax credit (1/9):	*£100*

Taxable dividend	*£1,000*

Income Tax thereon @ 10%	*£100*
Less tax credit:	*£100*

Income Tax payable	*Nil*
	=====

Effective tax rate on net dividend received: 0%

Ross, on the other hand, earns a good salary as a palaeontology professor and is therefore a higher rate taxpayer. The tax on his dividend is calculated as follows:

Dividend received:	*£900*
Plus tax credit (1/9):	*£100*

Taxable dividend	*£1,000*

Income Tax thereon @ 32.5%	*£325*
Less tax credit:	*£100*

Income Tax payable	*£225*
	=====

Effective tax rate on net dividend received: 25% (225/900)

So far, so good. Our example confirms that the actual tax rates for UK dividend income are 0% and 25%. It also confirms the fact that UK dividends are received tax free by basic rate taxpayers like Rachel.

We can also easily see that Ross and Rachel's marginal rate differential on dividend income is 25% – this is the saving which would be generated by moving dividend income from Ross to Rachel.

Now let's look at a slightly more complex example of marginal rate planning with dividends.

Example

Some years later, Rachel comes into a large inheritance and, in 2005/2006, she has UK dividend income of £27,000 and a capital gain of £20,000. Her tax bill for the year is calculated as follows:

Dividends	£27,000
Plus tax credits (1/9):	£3,000

Taxable dividends	£30,000
Income Tax thereon @ 10%	£3,000
Less tax credit:	£3,000

Income Tax payable on dividends	£0.00
Capital Gains	£20,000
Less Annual Exemption	£8,500

	£11,500
Capital Gains Tax @ 20% on remaining basic rate band (£37,295 - £30,000 = £7,295)	£1,459
Capital Gains Tax @ 40% on remaining capital gain of £4,205	£1,682
Total tax liability for the year	**£3,141**

Now, let's suppose for a moment that we are able to reduce Rachel's dividend income by £1,000. We must recalculate Rachel's tax in order to see what effect this has.

Example Continued

Rachel's tax liability for the year may be recalculated as follows:

Dividends	*£26,000*
Plus tax credits (1/9):	*£2,889*

Taxable dividends	*£28,889*
Income Tax thereon @ 10%	*£2,889*
Less tax credit:	*£2,889*

Income Tax payable on dividends	*£0.00*
Capital Gains	*£20,000*
Less Annual Exemption	*£8,500*

	£11,500
Capital Gains Tax @ 20% on remaining	
basic rate band (£37,295 - £28,889 = £8,406)	*£1,681.20*
Capital Gains Tax @ 40% on remaining	
£3,094	*£1,237.60*
Total tax liability for the year	**£2,918.80**

A reduction of £1,000 in Rachel's dividend income has saved her £222.20 in tax which means she has a marginal rate of 22.2%.

How does this come about? Her reduced income allows more of her capital gains to be taxed at 20% instead of 40%, a saving of 20%. The rather strange dividend tax credit system then multiplies this by 10/9 to give her a tax rate of 22.2%:

$$20\% \times 10/9 = 22.2\%$$

More importantly, what does this mean for Ross and Rachel's tax planning?

If Ross is a higher rate taxpayer with a 25% marginal rate on his dividend income, it would not be worth transferring any of Rachel's dividend income to him: His marginal rate is higher than Rachel's 22.2%

A small saving could, however, be made by transferring Ross's dividend income to Rachel, even though his total income for the year is actually less than her combined income and gains for the year.

Tax Tip

Tax savings are made by comparing marginal tax rates.

The partner with the highest overall income and gains does not necessarily have the highest marginal tax rate on all types of income.

Ignoring such quirks, when it comes to dividends the maximum tax that can be saved by moving UK dividend income from a higher rate taxpayer to a partner with no other income are as follows:

£33,565.50 @   25% (25% - 0%)   =   £8,391.38

In case you're wondering where the number £33,565.5 comes from, this is the amount of **net** dividends actually received which you can transfer to your partner. The gross dividend in your tax calculations would be £37,295 which is possibly a more familiar number – the income level where higher-rate tax kicks in.

The only way to get dividend income into a partner's hands is to make sure that they own the underlying shares on which the dividends are paid.

Quoted shares in listed companies can be given or sold to the partner. These transactions have various Capital Gains Tax and Inheritance Tax consequences which we will examine in Chapters 4, 7 and 10.

When it comes to private companies, we have a great many more options on how to get dividend income, as well as capital gains and other income, into the hands of a partner and we will return to this subject in Chapter 3.

2.13 FOREIGN DIVIDENDS

The UK tax system is pretty xenophobic and anything 'foreign' usually gets a different treatment to its UK equivalent.

Dividends are no exception since foreign dividends do not carry the one ninth tax credit which we saw in the previous section.

The UK tax payable on foreign dividends is therefore at the rates of Nil, 10% and 32.5%.

So, if a higher rate taxpayer moves foreign dividend income to their basic rate partner the couple could save Income Tax at 22.5% (32.5% - 10%).

In practice it can be a bit more complicated as you often have to pay *foreign* tax on foreign dividends. You can claim a deduction for this tax when you calculate your UK tax. This is called 'Double Tax Relief'.

The 'Double Tax Relief' cannot *exceed* the UK tax, in other words you cannot claim a repayment of the foreign tax you've paid.

Let's see how this works in an example.

Example

Asha receives a dividend of £750 from Brimful A.G., a Ruritanian company. The £750 received by Asha is net of Ruritanian withholding tax at 25%. Asha is a higher rate taxpayer. Her UK Income Tax liability on her Brimful dividends is thus calculated as follows:

Net dividend received:	*£750*
Foreign tax suffered:	*£250*

Taxable foreign dividend income:	*£1,000*

UK Income Tax @ 32.5%:	*£325*
Less Double Tax Relief	*£250*

UK Income Tax payable:	*£75*
	=====

As we can see, Asha's marginal rate of UK Income Tax on her Brimful A.G. dividends is only 7.5%!

What would happen if she were able to move this income to her *basic-rate* taxpayer partner?

Example Continued

Asha's partner Neeraj runs a local corner shop. This produces only a modest level of income meaning that he is a basic rate taxpayer.

His tax liability on the Brimful A.G. dividends is calculated as follows:

Net dividend received:	*£750*
Foreign tax suffered:	*£250*

Taxable foreign dividend income:	*£1,000*

UK Income Tax @ 10%:	*£100*
Less Double Tax Relief	*£100*

UK Income Tax payable:	*Nil*
	=====

Neeraj's Double Tax Relief is restricted to the amount of his UK tax liability on the same income and he is not entitled to any repayment of the foreign tax. His marginal rate of UK Income Tax on this income is therefore 0%.

The marginal rate differential on this income is therefore only 7.5%. Whilst the couple could save tax by moving this income to Neeraj, it is quite possible that there may be other income with a higher marginal rate differential which is available to utilise Neeraj's basic rate tax band and produce a greater overall tax saving.

The *maximum* annual UK tax savings achievable by moving foreign dividend income from a higher rate taxpayer to a partner with no other income and no Double Tax Relief are as follows:

£4,895	@	32.5%	(	32.5%	-	0%	)	=	£1,590.88
£32,400	@	22.5%	(	32.5%	-	10%	)	=	£7,290.00
								Total	£8,880.88

Moving foreign dividend income into a partner's hands will again mean ensuring that they own the relevant shares.

This, again, will usually have Capital Gains Tax and Inheritance Tax consequences, as described in later chapters. There may also be foreign tax implications to be considered and, if one of the partners is themselves non-UK resident or non-UK domiciled, the additional comments in Chapter 11 will be relevant.

2.14   RENTAL INCOME

To move rental income into the hands of a partner means transferring ownership of the property in its entirety or changing the ownership rights in jointly held property.

These complex matters are dependent on the couple's marital status and we will return to them in Chapters 4 and 7.

Many people with rental income will also have the ability to 'convert' their rental income into a different type of income for their partner. This is a subject which we will cover in Chapter 3.

For the moment though, it is simply worth noting that the maximum possible annual tax savings arising simply by moving rental income from a higher rate taxpayer partner to a partner with no other income are made up as follows:

£4,895	@	40%	(	40%	-	0%	)	=	£1,958.00
£2,090	@	30%	(	40%	-	10%	)	=	£627.00
£30,310	@	18%	(	40%	-	22%	)	=	£5,455.80
								Total	£8,040.80

2.15 EMPLOYMENT INCOME

Unless you have your own private company (which we shall come on to in Chapter 3), it is generally very difficult to move employment income.

Employment income, by its very nature, is personal in nature. There is no underlying asset which we can transfer to our partner in order to 'move' the income across to them.

One gentleman did once try to offset the cost of 'employing' his wife to clean his house and look after his children against his own, rather more substantial, employment income from his job in the City. Imaginative, but sadly not allowed!

In practice then, apart from couples with their own business, it is pretty rare to have a situation where a taxpayer is able to 'move' their employment income.

There are a few situations, however, where a couple may effectively share a job. Examples might include caretakers and couples who act as steward and cook at golf clubs or other private clubs.

Let's take a look at an example.

Example

For many years May has been employed to look after a country house. Her employer has been very generous and her annual salary is now £80,000.

In March 2005, May asks her employer if it would be alright for her young partner Lesley to move in with her. When they agree, May then asks if it would be alright for Lesley to share in some of the upkeep of the house and whether they would be amenable to paying Lesley a small salary and reducing May's own salary by the same amount.

Her employer is initially reluctant but May eventually manages to persuade them when she points out that there will be a £626.56 per year saving in employer's National Insurance.

Realising that May's plan has benefits for them too, her employer agrees that for the 2005/2006 tax year May will receive a salary of £42,705 and Lesley will receive a salary of £37,295 – just enough to use up all Lesley's basic-rate band.

The combined Income Tax and National Insurance suffered by the employed couple is thus as follows:

	May	*Lesley*
Salary	£42,705	£37,295
Less: Personal allowance	£4,895	£4,895
	£37,810	£32,400
Income Tax @ 10% on £2,090	£209.00	£209.00
Income Tax @ 22% on £30,310	£6,668.20	£6,668.20
Income Tax @ 40% on remainder	£2,164.00	-
National Insurance @ 11% on £27,865	£3,065.15	£3,065.15
National Insurance @ 1% on remainder	£99.45	£45.35
Total	**£12,205.80**	**£9,987.70**

To her considerable satisfaction May calculates that this has saved her and Lesley a total of £5,303.25 since Lesley's salary of £37,295 would otherwise have been taxed in May's hands at a combined rate of Income Tax and National Insurance of 41%.

This example is a good illustration of the maximum possible annual tax savings arising simply by moving employment income from a higher rate taxpayer partner to a partner with no other income. These savings are made up as follows:

£4,895	@	41%	(	41%	-	0%	)	=	£2,006.95
£2,090	@	20%	(	41%	-	21%	)	=	£418.00
£25,775	@	8%	(	41%	-	33%	)	=	£2,062.00
£4,535	@	18%	(	41%	-	23%	)	=	£816.30
							Total		£5,303.25

Plus, the following national insurance saving for the employer:

£4,895	@	12.8%	(	12.8%	-	0%	)	=	£626.56

But, of course, May was a pretty exceptional housekeeper and, in reality, a salary of £80,000 is not all that common.

Maybe so, but remember that thanks to national insurance an employee only has to earn over £6,985 before they are on a marginal rate of 33%. In a situation similar to May's, but with far less generous employers, transferring just £4,895 out of a salary of anything between £11,880 and £32,760 would produce a saving of £1,615.35 (£4,895 @ 33%) for the employee and still produces the same £626.56 saving for the employer.

Given that there is something in this for the boss, maybe you can find a job for your partner after all?

Before we leave employment income though, it's worth having a look at a little quirk in the tax system which is caused by National Insurance.

In the employment income table in Section 2.5 you can see that the marginal rate of Income Tax and National Insurance drops from 33% to 23% as your salary rises above £32,760.

This is because your income tax rate is still 22% but your national insurance rate falls from 11% to just 1%.

This is one of the few cases where your marginal tax rate actually **drops** as your income rises within the UK personal tax system and it gives us another interesting opportunity for some tax planning for couples with closely linked jobs.

Example

Richard and Julia are employed as the steward and cook in their local golf club. In 2004/2005, Richard receives a salary of £32,760 and Julia receives a salary of £11,520. From 6th April 2005, however, their salary structure is altered so that Richard's income rises to £37,295 and Julia only receives £6,985. Their combined Income Tax and National Insurance Contributions for 2005/2006 will therefore now be as follows:

	Julia	*Richard*
Salary	*£6,985*	*£37,295*
Less: Personal allowance	*£4,895*	*£4,895*
	£2,090	*£32,400*
Income Tax @ 10% on £2,090	*£209.00*	*£209.00*
Income Tax @ 22% on £30,310	*-*	*£6,668.20*
National Insurance @ 11% on £2,090	*£229.9*	*-*
National Insurance @ 11% on £27,865	*-*	*£3,065.15*
National Insurance @ 1% on £4,535	*-*	*£45.35*
Total	**£438.9**	**£9,987.70**

This saves the couple a total of £453.50 as income of £4,535 has been moved from a marginal rate of 33% in Julia's hands to a rate of only 23% in Richard's hands. The couple have therefore utilised a marginal rate differential of 10% to their advantage.

The method described above would have worked just as well as long as the less well paid member of the couple started out with a salary of anything up to £32,760. We should stop once we have moved enough income to the better paid partner to bring them up to a salary of £37,295, however, as their marginal rate then increases to 41%.

This is a quite exceptional case where moving income from the partner with less income to the partner with higher income will actually save tax.

2.16 CAPITAL GAINS

Capital Gains Tax planning is a huge subject in its own right. We have already touched on it once or twice in the preceding sections and we will also see it again in later chapters.

As far as the principle of sharing a couple's wealth is concerned, the key is to ensure that both of their Capital Gains Tax reliefs and exemptions are utilised as far as possible.

To get capital gains into a partner's hands must inevitably mean getting the relevant asset, or a share of the relevant asset, into their hands somehow. This may be by transferring assets, or shares of assets, or assigning rights over assets, to a partner prior to selling them.

In cases of more forward planning it means ensuring that a low-taxed partner holds the asset from the outset.

As usual, any transfers will generally have their own tax implications and, as usual, these will depend on the couple's marital status so we will be looking at them in later chapters.

There is, however, one very important overriding principle that applies to Capital Gains Tax planning for *all* couples.

In order to ensure that a capital gain is taxed in your partner's hands, they must have 'beneficial' ownership of the relevant asset prior to its subsequent disposal to a third party. This is vital.

For them to obtain beneficial ownership of the asset it must be theirs to do with as they wish.

This means that the partner who does the transfer must not retain any rights which would prevent the other partner from doing as they wish with the asset.

It must also mean that there is not already an existing commitment to sell the asset to someone else. Many people doing last minute tax planning slip up in this respect.

If the asset is already effectively 'sold' then the transferee partner will never have acquired beneficial ownership, as the ultimate purchaser now has the beneficial interest. Any supposed transfer to the partner will therefore be ineffective for Capital Gains Tax purposes.

Wealth Warning

Transfers of assets to a partner for Capital Gains Tax planning purposes must take place *before* there is any commitment to sell the asset.

Determining when exactly a 'commitment' to sell is in place will depend on the facts of the individual case.

The existence of a sale contract (or missives in Scotland) will almost certainly mean that this commitment exists.

Sometimes, even a less formal arrangement is evidence enough of a commitment so that a transferee partner does not obtain beneficial ownership.

There is sometimes even a degree of doubt as soon as an asset has been 'put on the market'.

Tax Tip

The general rule of thumb regarding transfers of assets to a partner for Capital Gains Tax planning purposes is to do them as early as possible and preferably before any attempt is made to sell the asset. Do remember to check the tax implications of the transfer to your partner first though.

The Annual Exemption

Most commonly, couples save Capital Gains Tax by ensuring that they each use their annual exemptions. At its current level of £8,500, the annual exemption provides a simple opportunity to save up to £3,400 in Capital Gains Tax (because £8,500 x 40% tax = £3,400).

The motto for the annual exemption is 'Use It Or Lose It'.

Hence, any tax planning which utilises a partner's annual exemption is generally pretty sound.

Lower and Basic Rate Tax Bands

In many other cases, a partner's lower and basic rate tax bands will also be available.

Capital gains falling within these bands are taxed at 10% and 20% respectively.

At first glance, therefore, it would appear that it would always be beneficial to move any capital gains from the hands of a 40% taxpayer into the hands of a partner taxed at 10% or 20%.

However, there are cases where the higher rate taxpayer partner will actually have a *lower* effective rate of Capital Gains Tax than their basic rate or lower rate taxpayer partner.

Most such cases arise due to the availability of taper relief.

Taper relief can result in a higher rate taxpayer having an effective Capital Gains Tax rate of only 10% and moving gains to a basic rate taxpayer in these circumstances could be disadvantageous.

Another important area is that of principal private residence relief and Private Letting Relief. Both of these apply in the case of a sale of a property which is, or has been, your main residence, i.e. your home.

These reliefs can again result in one partner having a lower marginal rate of Capital Gains Tax than we might have expected and must also be taken into account before transferring a capital gain into the hands of a supposedly low-taxed partner.

Principal private residence relief and its partner in crime, Private Letting Relief, are dependent on a couple's marital status, so we shall return to this topic in later chapters.

'Normal' Maximum Saving

Leaving these special cases to one side for the time being, however, the maximum annual Capital Gains Tax saving which can normally be achieved by moving fully taxable capital gains, where no other reliefs are available, from a higher rate taxpayer partner to a partner with income not exceeding the personal allowance is as follows:

£8,500	@	40%	(	40%	-	0%	)	=	£3,400.00
£2,090	@	30%	(	40%	-	10%	)	=	£627.00
£30,310	@	20%	(	40%	-	20%	)	=	£6,062.00
							Total		£10,089.00

2.17   CAPITAL LOSSES

Capital losses are not transferable so the general tax planning idea is to get capital gains into the hands of the partner who has the capital losses.

Brought Forward Capital Losses

As far as capital losses brought forward from earlier tax years are concerned, the only way to utilise these is to ensure that the same person who has the losses realises some taxable capital gains.

This is a tricky thing to organise at the best of times but as a couple you may sometimes be able to plan your affairs to get the best out of your capital losses without altering your investment strategy.

It can be very difficult to ensure that you get the best value from your capital losses.

There is a complex interplay between capital losses, taper relief and the annual exemption, meaning that capital losses may only produce savings at 10% or may even be wasted altogether.

This is especially the case where one partner qualifies for business asset taper relief but the other partner doesn't. This is often the case when buying shares in the company that employs you.

You might remember from the terminology section 1.3 that taper relief reduces your taxable profits the longer you hold an asset. Business asset taper relief is very generous and exempts 75% of your profits after just two years. It applies to certain types of commercial property and many shares owned by company employees.

As a general guide, the best strategy is to try to get investments which will **not** be eligible for business asset taper relief into the hands of the partner with brought forward capital losses.

The other partner then makes the investments which will attract business asset taper relief.

Current Year Capital Losses

Any capital losses which you make in the *current* tax year will automatically be set off against your total capital gains in the current tax year. This set off takes place before you calculate taper relief and deduct the annual exemption.

Couples should therefore try to avoid wasting their annual exemptions through the automatic set off of current year capital losses.

Here is how a couple with a mixture of capital gains and capital losses in the current year, should ideally try to organise them:

Net Losses or Net Gains Less Than £17,000

Let's say, as a couple, you anticipate making an overall loss or you anticipate making gains of less than £17,000 (twice the annual exemption), after all reliefs and after deducting capital losses

In this case try to ensure that one partner has taxable capital gains equal to the £8,500 annual exemption.

This will maximise the net capital loss which the *other* partner can carry forward.

Net Gains Greater Than Two Annual Exemptions

If, as a couple, your total net taxable capital gains after all reliefs and after deducting capital losses *will* amount to more than twice the annual exemption, try to ensure that the excess (but no more) falls on the partner with the lowest marginal rate of Capital Gains Tax.

If one partner has brought forward capital losses then they should be regarded as having a marginal rate Capital Gains Tax rate of 0%.

If both partners are already higher rate taxpayers then your only priority is to ensure that both annual exemptions are fully utilised.

2.18   WHEN EQUALITY IS NOT THE BEST POLICY

Earlier on I said that sharing everything equally was a good general rule of thumb, but that it wasn't foolproof.

Having covered capital losses, this gives me the opportunity to point out a situation where sharing everything equally is not to a couple's best advantage.

Suppose that a couple buy two lots of shares and in 2005/2006 one of these investments yields a capital gain of £4,000 each and the other yields a capital loss of £4,000 each.

Each partner will have a net capital gain for the year of nil.

However, if only one partner had bought the profitable shares, their net capital gain would be £8,000. This would be covered by the annual exemption so there would still be no Capital Gains Tax payable. Fine.

The other partner would have a capital loss of £8,000 to carry forward with a future tax saving potential of up to £3,200. Fine and dandy.

So, you see, equality is not <u>always</u> the best policy.

We've got another example of the occasional benefits of inequality coming up in the next section too.

2.19   CHILDREN'S TAX CREDITS

Generally speaking, when undertaking any tax planning, it is also wise to take any impact on the taxpayer's tax credit claim into account, if applicable.

All co-habiting couples have always had to make their tax credit claims based on *total* household income.

Because the claim is based on combined household income most couples' tax credit claims will be unaffected by any tax planning strategies involving moving wealth from one partner to the other.

One exception to this rule is partners who regard themselves as a couple but who are not co-habiting.

Example

Chris and Sam regard themselves as a couple but live in separate houses.

Together they run a florist business called ChrisSamthamums, which makes a steady annual profit of £150,000. Up until now, they have been sharing this profit equally.

Sam has a young baby and is thus entitled to a maximum 'Baby Tax Credit' of £1,090. If, however, Sam received the usual equal profit share of £75,000, all of this entitlement would be withdrawn.

Chris and Sam therefore alter their profit share to a 2 to 1 ratio in favour of Chris. This reduces Sam's income for the year to £50,000, thus ensuring that the couple continue to benefit from the £1,090 Baby Tax Credit.

Chris and Sam's saving springs from the fact that the family element of Child Tax Credit is withdrawn at the rate of £1 for every additional £15 of income over £50,000.

The family element of Child Tax Credit is currently £545. The family element is doubled to £1,090 when the household includes a child under the age of one in the relevant tax year, as in Sam's case. This is sometimes referred to as 'Baby Tax Credit'.

Hence, in a situation like Chris and Sam's the usual marginal rate tax planning principles apply and we can therefore save tax credits by moving income out of a claimant's hands and into their partner's.

Remember though, that we were only able to do this because Chris and Sam were **not** co-habiting.

For couples on lower levels of income who are entitled to working tax credits and/or child tax credits, this type of planning will be much more important where it is applicable. It can produce a total effective marginal rate of as much as **70%** in some cases! (This is the combined rate of Income Tax, National Insurance and tax credit withdrawal.)

2.20   THE ULTIMATE COUPLES TAX SAVING PLAN

In sections 2.11 to 2.16, I provided an analysis of the maximum annual saving achievable simply by moving various types of income or capital gains.

In the right circumstances, however, even greater savings are achievable by moving different combinations of income types and gains.

The Ultimate Couples Tax Saving Plan Example

Chandler has a part-time job as a caretaker with annual pay of £11,880. He also has a small business which produces an annual profit of £8,688. Mostly, however, he lives off his investment income. He receives UK dividends of £48,620 and always makes capital gains of at least £17,000 each year. His tax bill would be calculated as follows:

	£

Employment Income - £11,880
£11,880 less £4,895 personal allowance
leaves £6,985 taxable

	£
Income Tax @ 10% on £2,090	209.00
Income Tax @ 22% on £4,895	1,076.90
National Insurance @ 11% on £6,985	768.35

Trading Income - £8,688

Income Tax @ 22%	1,911.36

£8,688 less national insurance
lower earning limit of £4,895 leaves
£3,793 subject to national insurance

Class 4 National Insurance @ 8% on £3,793	303.44
Class 2 National Insurance @ £2.10 per week	109.20

UK Dividend Income - £48,620
Add Tax Credit @ 1/9 = £5,402.22
Results in taxable dividend of £54,022.22

Income Tax @ 10% on remaining basic rate band (£37,295 – £11,880 - £8,688 = £16,727)	1,672.70
Income Tax @ 32.5% on remainder	12,120.95
Less Dividend Tax Credit	-5,402.22

Capital Gains - £17,000
Less £8,500 exemption leaves £8,500 taxable

Capital Gains Tax @ 40% on £8,500	3,400.00
Total Tax for the Year:	**16,169.68**

Like many people Chandler hadn't realised just how much tax he was actually paying until his friend Joey sat him down one evening and worked it out for him. Knowing that Chandler's partner Monica had no income of her own, Joey suggested the following changes.

"Firstly", says Joey, "get her to share your caretaking job."

"Actually", admits Chandler, "she does most of it already."

"Fine", says Joey, "see if you can get them to put her on a salary of £4,895 and drop yours by the same amount. They should be happy 'cause it'll save them £626.56 too. You save Income Tax at 22% and National Insurance at 11% and she gets the money tax free."

"Why not give her the whole salary?" asks Chandler.

"No, you don't want to do that. If you pass over any more than £4,895, she'll have to start paying National Insurance.

Next, you want to take her into partnership with you in the business. Give her an equal share which will be £4,344 and therefore below the small earnings exception."

"But I thought she'd have to start paying National Insurance if she got any more earnings?" queries Chandler.

"No, that's OK", Joey assures him, "it's a different class of National Insurance for business income. She doesn't have to pay any 'Class 4' or 'Class 2' National Insurance if we keep her income from the business under £4,345. This also takes your business income under £4,345 too, so you won't have to pay any Class 2 any more either."

"Won't that ruin my state pension?"

Joey shows Chandler a book and points him to section 12.4, which satisfies Chandler's concerns about state pensions.

"Then all you have to do is to make sure that she gets £25,250 out of your dividends and £8,500 of your capital gains." Joey finishes.

Joey then shows Chandler what his 2005/2006 tax bill would look like if he made these changes:

	£

Employment Income - £6,985
Less £4,895 personal allowance
leaves £2,090 taxable

Income Tax @ 10%	209.00
National Insurance @ 11%	229.90

Partnership Trading Income - £4,344

Income Tax @ 22%	955.68
No National Insurance	

UK Dividend Income - £23,370.00
Add Tax Credit @ 1/9 = £2,596.67
Results in taxable dividend of £25,966.67

Income Tax @ 10% on remaining basic	
rate band (£37,295 – £6,985 - £4,344 = £25,966)	2,596.60
Income Tax @ 32.5% on remaining £0.67	0.22
Less Dividend Tax Credit	-2,596.67

Capital Gains - £8,500
Less annual exemption

Leaves £0 taxable	0

Total Tax for the year:	**£1,394.73**

"That's great", says Chandler. "But what about Monica's tax?"

Joey then produces the corresponding calculation for Monica, as follows:

	£
Employment Income - £4,895	
Less £4,895 personal allowance	0
Partnership Trading Income - £4,344	
Income Tax @ 10% on £2,090	209.00
Income Tax @ 22% on remaining £2,254	495.88
No National Insurance Contributions payable	
UK Dividend Income - £25,250.00	
Add Tax Credit @ 1/9ⁿ = £2,805.55	
Results in taxable dividend of £28,055.55	
All within remaining basic rate band	
(£37,295 – £4,895 - £4,344 = £28,056)	
Therefore, Income Tax @ 10% =	2,805.55
Less Dividend Tax Credit	-2,805.55
Capital Gains - £8,500	
Less annual exemption	
Leaves £0 taxable	0
Total Tax Liability for the year:	**704.88**

"Wow", exclaims Chandler, "you mean our total combined tax bill for the year will only be £2,099.61 instead of £16,169.68. You've saved us over £14,000!"

"£14,070.07 to be precise" confirms a rather smug Joey. "You're just lucky that you happen to be in the perfect situation to save lots of tax."

"Is there anything else you can do?" asks Chandler.

"Well, if I can get you to have a baby and then live apart afterwards, I can get you another £1,090. If you remember the national insurance saving that your boss is also making, that brings us to a grand total of £15,786.63 and I think that's about the best that I can do."

People in Chandler and Monica's exact circumstances are, of course, pretty rare, so achieving the 'ultimate' couples tax saving plan is also going to be a pretty rare event. Nevertheless, I would hope that this example provides a flavour of what marginal rate tax planning is really capable of achieving.

We touched on some business tax planning issues in this example too and I will explain these in more depth in the next chapter.

But, before we leave the ultimate couple's tax saving plan, let's look at how Joey achieves this amazing saving:

- First, we have the £4,895 of employment income moved to Monica. Chandler was paying 22% Income Tax and 11% National Insurance on this income, a total of 33%.

  This income is tax free in Monica's hands because it is less than her personal allowance.

- Furthermore, as a result of this income switch more of Chandler's dividend income drops into his own basic rate band and that income becomes tax free instead of being taxed at 25%.

- Next Chandler transfers £2,090 of trading income. He was paying combined Income Tax and National Insurance at 30% on this income, but Monica will pay just 10% in Income Tax, a saving of 20%.

- In addition, £2,090 of Chandler's dividend income drops into his basic-rate band and becomes tax free.

- A further £1,703 of the transferred trading income was also being taxed at a combined rate of 30% in Chandler's hands but Monica will pay 22% in Income Tax on this sum. This direct tax saving is increased, again, by a tax saving on Chandler's dividend income.

- Lastly, there is a final £551 of trading income on which Chandler would have paid 22% Income Tax, but so will Monica. What the transfer of this final bit of trading income does achieve though is exempting Chandler from Class 2 National Insurance Contributions which would have amounted to £109.20 a year. The transfer also produces the usual indirect saving on his dividend income.

- All of the dividend income that Chandler transfers to Monica was being taxed at 25% but now becomes tax free, producing a tax saving at an effective rate of 25%.

- The transferred capital gains save Capital Gains Tax at the rate of 40%.

I hope that this example demonstrates marginal rate planning for couples in action and shows how taking each partner's overall position fully into account is essential to getting the best out of the situation.

You and your partner's own personal 'ultimate' savings plan will be unique to you and will be achieved by following the six step plan which I set out in section 2.7.

2.21 TIMING IS EVERYTHING

Another common theme to the tax planning techniques available to couples is the ability to **control the timing of transactions**. This is often of most use in the field of Capital Gains Tax planning.

Sometimes there is an advantage to creating a disposal of an asset **now** in order to fully enjoy the benefits of various tax exemptions and reliefs which are 'time sensitive' and may therefore either diminish or be lost altogether. These include:

- The annual Capital Gains Tax exemption
- Business Asset Taper Relief for Capital Gains Tax
- The Principal Private Residence exemption (for a former home)

Having a partner allows you to maximize these reliefs quite easily: You simply sell the asset to your partner – a 'friendly' deal which can usually be done pretty quickly.

This means the asset will still be under the couple's control, which is particularly useful when we want to maximise the tax benefits without actually losing the underlying asset. In tax planning we often refer to this as 'crystallising a gain' – i.e. causing a capital gain to arise without actually disposing of the asset.

Most tax planning techniques revolving around transfers of assets between partners are very much dependent on the couple's legal status, so we shall return to this theme in later chapters.

'Bed and breakfasting' is, however, one variation on this theme which is generally available to all couples, as we shall see in the next section.

2.22   BED AND BREAKFASTING

In the good old days, taxpayers with stock market investment portfolios were able to utilise their annual Capital Gains Tax exemptions without having to relinquish the long-term growth prospects of their investments. They simply sold enough shares one day to create sufficient capital gains to utilise their annual exemption and then bought the same shares back the next morning.

The reason people did this was because of our annual exemption motto: 'Use It Or Lose It'.

Naturally, there were always costs involved but these were usually far outweighed by the tax savings.

To avoid too much risk of price movements, the sale was usually done as late as possible before the markets closed and the repurchase carried out first thing the following morning. Hence the term 'bed and breakfast'.

Sadly, some anti-avoidance legislation brought in a few years ago means that individuals are no longer able to carry out 'bed and breakfasting' on their own.

Being in a couple, however, means that we can still carry out 'bed and breakfasting' with one slight refinement. The only change required to make 'bed and breakfasting' work nowadays is that one partner sells the relevant investments and the other partner buys them back.

Any couple can do this but married couples and registered civil partners must be careful not to make a direct sale from one partner to the other or else the 'bed and breakfasting' simply won't work as desired. In the case of stock market investments, this doesn't cause any problems, as the sale and subsequent repurchase take place on the open market.

The other advantage which couples have is that they don't even have to wait overnight like the old 'bed and breakfast' scheme – one partner's purchase can take place on the same day as the other partner's sale.

Here is a simple example of how 'bed and breakfasting' works and why you might want to do it.

Example

Phoebe is a higher rate taxpayer. She has 10,000 shares in Growfast plc which she bought for £1 each in December 2005. By the end of March 2006, they are already worth £2 each and still going up in value fast. She doesn't want to lose out on the potential growth in her investment but also doesn't want to waste her annual Capital Gains Tax exemption.

On 4th April 2006 Phoebe sells 8,500 Growfast plc shares for £17,000. On the same day, her partner Mike buys 8,500 Growfast plc shares on the stock market.

Phoebe has a capital gain of £8,500 for 2005/2006 but this is covered by her annual exemption so there is no tax.

Twelve months later, Growfast plc is being quoted at £3.0353 each so, on 2nd April 2007, Mike sells his 8,500 shares to give him a 2006/2007 capital gain of £8,800. This gain is covered by Mike's 2006/2007 annual exemption which is now worth £8,800. Again there is no Capital Gains Tax to pay.

On the same day that Mike sells his shares, Phoebe buys 8,500 Growfast plc shares on the stock market at a cost of £25,800.

In May 2007, Growfast plc announces that it has won a major new contract and the price of its shares shoots up to £10 each. At this point, Phoebe decides to sell up.

If Phoebe and Mike had never carried out the bed and breakfasting, Phoebe's capital gain would have been £90,000 with a Capital Gains Tax bill of £32,360.

Instead, however, her Capital Gains Tax computation is as follows:

Sale proceeds	*£100,000*
Less purchase costs:	
December 2005 (remaining 1,500 shares)	*£1,500*
April 2007	*£25,800*

	£72,700
Less 2007/2008 annual exemption	*£9,100*

	£63,600
	=======

Her Capital Gains Tax liability will therefore be only £25,440, meaning that the 'bed and breakfasting' has made her a net saving of £6,920.

As I mentioned above, there are costs involved in carrying out 'bed and breakfasting', such as stamp duty. Generally though, these costs will themselves be allowable deductions for Capital Gains Tax purposes.

Taper Relief

The impact of taper relief must also be taken into account when doing bed and breakfasting.

Taper relief is applied before the annual exemption. So if you have some shares which you've held for just over four years they'll qualify for 10% taper relief.

This means you can make a capital gain of £9,444 which will still be totally covered by your 2005/2006 annual exemption:

£9,444 – 10% = £8,500

When carrying out bed and breakfasting therefore, the amount of capital gain which may be covered by your annual exemption will be increased if the assets enjoy taper relief.

For the 2005/2006 tax year, the maximum amounts of capital gain before taper relief which may be covered by the annual exemption are as follows:

	Taper Relief	Maximum Gain Covered by Annual Exemption
Business Assets		
Held for one year, but less than two	50%	£17,000
Held for two years or more	75%	£34,000
Other assets		
Held for three years, but less than four	5%	£8,947
Held for four years, but less than five	10%	£9,444
Held for five years, but less than six	15%	£10,000
Held for six years, but less than seven	20%	£10,625
Held for seven years, but less than eight & not since before 17/3/1998	25%	£11,333
Held for eight years or since before 17/3/1998	30%	£12,142

Note that, in the above tables, we are assuming that the partner selling the assets has no other capital gains in the same tax year.

Appendix E provides a brief summary of the types of assets which qualify as business assets for taper relief purposes. This is, however, a complex matter and professional advice should always be sought before assuming that any asset will necessarily qualify as a business asset.

Beware, however, that carrying out 'bed and breakfasting' means that the partner who has newly acquired the relevant assets will not themselves initially be entitled to any taper relief. They will have to wait the relevant period before the taper relief is recovered. In some instances, this could backfire badly!

Example

Dave has some quoted shares in Oopsadaisy plc worth £100,000 which are eligible for taper relief at 75% and which he bought some years ago for £65,670 plus Stamp Duty of £330.

Dave and his partner Sam decide to do some 'bed and breakfasting' so, in late March 2006, Dave sells his shares and, on the same day, Sam buys an equivalent number of shares on the open market for £100,000.

Dave makes a capital gain of £34,000, reduced by taper relief to £8,500, which, of course, is covered by his annual exemption.

Quite unexpectedly, in February 2007 Oopsadaisy plc is bought out by Massive Conglomerate Inc. Sam receives £250,000 in exchange for the shares which were 'bed and breakfasted' the previous March. Because he has held them for less than a year he doesn't qualify for any taper relief.

*Let's now look at Sam's Capital Gains Tax calculation, as well as what Dave's would have been if they **hadn't** carried out the 'bed and breakfasting' in March 2006.*

	Sam	**Dave**
Sale Proceeds	*£250,000*	*£250,000*
Less:		
Share purchase cost	*£100,000*	*£65,670*
Stamp Duty on purchase	*£500*	*£330*
	£149,500	*£184,000*
Taper Relief @ Nil/75%	*-*	*£138,000*
	£149,500	*£46,000*
Less 2006/2007 annual exemption	*£8,800*	*£8,800*
	£140,700	*£37,200*
Capital Gains Tax payable	*£56,280*	*£14,880*

Oops! That's what I call backfiring. Their 'bed and breakfast' planning has cost Sam and Dave £41,400 in extra Capital Gains Tax.

"Well, who was to know that Oopsadaisy plc would get bought out?", I hear you ask. This is true, but that's just the point – how do any of us ever know what tomorrow will bring.

All I can say is that you just have to be aware that this sort of thing can happen.

Capital Losses & Bed and Breakfasting

Another factor which may potentially have an impact on your 'bed and breakfasting' will be the presence of any capital losses which either partner may have, either brought forward from previous years, or within the same tax year.

As far as capital losses arising within the same tax year are concerned, a 'bed and breakfast' type transaction is a good way to ensure that the losses do not result in the loss-making partner's annual exemption being wasted.

Example

Munro has made capital losses of £5,000 already this tax year and has also made capital gains of £8,500.

The capital gains would be tax free thanks to Munro's annual exemption but he will be forced to set off his current year capital losses first, thus wasting £5,000 of his annual exemption.

Munro has some other quoted shares which have made some good profits but he doesn't want to sell them.

What he can do is enter into a 'bed and breakfast' type transaction by selling enough of the other shares to yield a £5,000 gain. Munro's partner Marilyn will then buy an equivalent number of the same shares on the open market and thus ensure that the couple still hold the same investment.

This will ensure that Munro's annual exemption is fully utilised and the benefit of his £5,000 capital losses has not been wasted.

A similar technique can be used to get better value out of brought forward capital losses. We will look at an example of this in the next section.

2.23   PARTNERS WITH A SPECIAL TAX STATUS

In section 2.7, I gave you the general rule of thumb that a couple will usually optimise the use of their tax exemptions and reliefs if they share all of their wealth equally.

I did say that it wasn't foolproof though and we've already seen a few exceptions to this rule.

A further major exception occurs whenever one partner has some kind of special tax status which the other does not have. In such cases, it will obviously make sense to maximise the benefit of that partner's special status.

The main instances of 'special tax status' are where one partner, but not the other, is:

- Non-UK resident
- Non-UK domiciled
- Over state retirement age
- Eligible for principal private residence relief on a property
- Eligible for business asset taper relief on an asset
- A crown servant, or member of the diplomatic service, or
- A member of the armed forces.

Couples with one partner falling under points one or two above have the potential for significant additional areas of tax planning and we will deal with these in Chapter 11.

Having one member of the couple over state retirement age provides the possibility for a little extra tax planning and we will cover this in Chapter 9.

Principal private residence relief is so dependent on marital status that we will have to come back to it later.

It is vitally important to be aware of each partner's tax status for business asset taper relief purposes as this can make the difference between an effective rate of Capital Gains Tax of 10% and an effective rate of 40%.

But what if you find that an asset is already growing in value in one partner's hands when the other partner is the one who would be eligible for business asset taper relief?

In many cases, the answer to this will depend on the couple's marital status so we shall return to this problem later.

Any couple, however, could use 'bed and breakfasting' to move assets across to the partner with the better potential taper relief rate.

2.24   STAMP DUTY & STAMP DUTY LAND TAX

Whatever your marital status, there are no special exemptions for Stamp Duty or Stamp Duty Land Tax on transfers of assets to your partner. If you sell any shares to your partner, they will have to pay Stamp Duty at 0.5%, rounded up to the nearest £5.

If you sell property to your partner for more than £120,000 (or £150,000 for commercial property), they will have to pay Stamp Duty Land Tax of at least 1% of the sale price and perhaps as much as 3% or 4% for a larger property.

However, in many cases, such transfers tend to be gifts, with no purchase consideration being paid. Both Stamp Duty on shares and Stamp Duty Land Tax on land and property are based on the actual consideration paid (unlike most other taxes where market value must often be substituted for the actual price).

Hence, in the case of gifts to your partner, neither Stamp Duty nor Stamp Duty Land Tax will generally be payable.

Wealth Warning

Where a transferee assumes any liabilities (e.g. a mortgage) on the transfer of an asset, this will be deemed to be consideration paid for Stamp Duty or Stamp Duty Land Tax purposes. The marital status of the transferor and transferee makes no difference.

Example

Kirk has a small flat in London worth £300,000 with an outstanding mortgage of £130,000. He gives the flat to his partner Burt, who takes over the mortgage.

Burt is deemed to have paid £130,000 for the flat and is therefore liable for Stamp Duty Land Tax at 1%, i.e. £1,300.

Tax Tip

Note that, if Kirk had paid off £10,000 of the mortgage before the transfer, Burt's deemed payment would have been reduced to £120,000 and the transfer would then be exempt from Stamp Duty Land Tax.

Chapter 3

Couples In Business

3.1 WHY ARE COUPLES IN BUSINESS A SPECIAL CASE?

Any couple where one or both of the partners have their own business has the opportunity to undertake further areas of tax planning not generally available to other couples.

Not only can these couples 'move' income more effectively, they can also often 'convert' income from one type to another.

Example

Goldie runs a small shoe shop as a sole trader.

Her partner Kurt does a few odd jobs in the shop from time to time for which she pays him a salary of £4,895 per annum.

By paying Kurt a salary of £4,895, Goldie has effectively converted some of her self-employment income into employment income in Kurt's hands.

This income is covered by Kurt's personal allowance and is tax free.

So, yes, couples in business are very much a special case.

3.2 WHEN IS A COUPLE IN BUSINESS?

As far as this guide is concerned, we will define a 'couple in business' as any couple where one or both of them is:

- A sole trader,
- In a business partnership,
- A director or shareholder of a private company, or
- Has a property business (i.e. has rental income).

Each of these provides its own tax planning opportunities which we shall look at in turn.

When it comes to business partnerships things may get a little confusing as we will be talking about 'partners' where one has a personal relationship, as well as 'business partners' and 'business partnerships' which are business relationships and not personal relationships. To compound matters, our personal partner may sometimes also be our business partner.

In an attempt to make matters clearer, therefore, I will always use the terms 'business partner' and 'business partnership' where relevant. If I refer simply to a 'partner' I am talking about your personal relationship partner.

Before we move on to the various types of business structures, however, let's start by taking a closer look at one aspect of tax planning for couples in business which is common to all of the above business types: paying your partner a salary.

3.3   PAYING YOUR PARTNER A SALARY

Where only one partner in a couple is in business – regardless of what legal structure is being used – paying a salary to the other partner is very often an effective tax saving measure.

Using The Partner's Personal Allowance

If the other partner has no other income, a salary of up to the level of their £4,895 personal allowance will be free from both Income Tax and National Insurance.

This could save the partner who is in business anything up to the following amounts:

- Sole traders: £2,006.95
- Those in a business partnership: £2,006.95
- Those with their own private company: £1,603.11 for the company, or
- If used to reduce their own salary: £2,633.51

And these savings do not take account of any *additional* savings caused by pushing any other non-business income of the employer partner into a lower tax bracket (in other words, where that partner has one of the marginal rates of 42% or more which we saw in Chapter 2).

Sometimes the 'employee' partner has a little investment income, so the 'employer' partner pays them something less than the full amount of the personal allowance so that the employee partner doesn't wind up with a tax liability. This is not always the best marginal rate tax planning but it keeps life simple.

Simple and Foolproof?

In any circumstances where the salary is tax free in the employee partner's hands, the payment of that salary to them will seem like a pretty simple and foolproof piece of tax planning.

Simple? Well, reasonably. Strictly, the employer partner must put their employee partner on the payroll and produce all of the usual PAYE returns as for any other employee. The fact that no PAYE or National Insurance is payable on such a small salary does not alter this fact. Before you grumble about this piece of 'mindless bureaucracy', however, I must again point you to section 12.4, where you will see that it may have its advantages.

If your partner is your first or only employee, this will mean that you should register as an employer with Revenue & Customs under the PAYE system.

As for foolproof? Definitely not, I'm afraid.

The first question is whether a £4,895 salary payment to the partner is justified. The second question, thanks to the national minimum wage rules is whether it should, in fact, be more!

Is a Salary Payment Justified?

This piece of tax planning is so simple and so effective that almost every person in business whose partner is not in paid employment pays that partner a small salary.

But, creating income for your partner is the easy part. To make the tax planning work, you also need to be able to claim a deduction for your partner's salary as a business expense.

This deduction is not automatic – the payment must be made 'wholly and exclusively for the benefit of the trade or business' before it is properly deductible. In other words, the employee partner must be doing sufficient work for the business to justify a salary of £4,895.

What you need to ask yourself before you make a claim for your partner's salary, therefore, is whether you'd be prepared to pay someone else, with whom you have no personal relationship, the same amount of money for the same amount of work.

Kurt, as we saw in the example in section 3.1, did some maintenance work in Goldie's shop and hence the payment to him was probably a justifiable business expense.

Very often, the partner will do some of the paperwork for the business and they will receive a salary for that. Most businesses produce enough paperwork to justify a salary level of at least £4,895, although there are exceptions.

Sometimes though, the partner at home is apparently paid £4,895 for 'answering the phone and taking messages'. That may be alright if the business is run from home but, if there are completely separate office premises, this will not generally be sufficient to justify that level of salary.

Another ploy I have often seen is that the partner is paid to 'entertain customers at home'. Again, this is unlikely to justify a salary of £4,895. This one is probably the weakest argument of all, in fact, as it is generally pretty unlikely that the partner with the business would actually pay an unconnected third party for these services. Entertaining customers at home is usually seen by Revenue & Customs as simply part of a partner's normal, private, role.

Having said all that, just because a salary of £4,895 cannot be justified, this doesn't stop you from paying a smaller, more reasonable level of salary, where this can be justified as a proper business expense.

If, as in many cases, a marginal rate tax saving of 41% is at stake than even a salary of £1,000 will provide an annual saving of £410 and that is still worthwhile.

The Impact of The National Minimum Wage

On 1st October 2005, the national minimum wage for workers aged 22 or over was raised from £4.85 per hour to £5.05 per hour.

The rate for those aged 18 to 21, and for older workers undergoing accredited training within the first six months of a new employment, was also raised from £4.10 per hour to £4.25 per hour.

There are no exceptions from the national minimum wage just because the employee happens to also be your partner, even if they are your legally married spouse or registered civil partner.

Hence, if your partner is also your employee and they carry out a substantial amount of work for your business, you may find that you are actually obliged to pay them more than the personal allowance.

At the main national minimum wage rate, the £4,895 personal allowance equates to just over 969 hours work in a year. That's equivalent to a little over 18 and a half hours per week.

In many cases, where the employee partner only works for their partner's business part-time, the national minimum wage will therefore not be a problem.

On the other hand, if your partner works as an employee of your business full-time, say 40 hours per week, then strictly they should be receiving an annual salary of £10,504, which is well over the personal allowance.

Whilst I haven't yet seen many cases of the national minimum wage being enforced in the case of a business owner's partner, this nevertheless is what the law says and Revenue & Customs will use any aspect of the law that they can when it is to their advantage.

Beyond the Personal Allowance

Having looked at why you might *have* to pay your partner a salary above the personal allowance, we also need to consider whether you might actually *want* to.

There are some good non-tax reasons why you would pay your partner a more commercial level of salary, including pension entitlement, mortgage applications and prestige. You may also simply want to show your appreciation of the work they do. Sometimes also, although they may be your partner, you will want their salary to operate within the same pay structure as other employees.

These are all good reasons, but we're here to talk about tax.

When it comes to paying your partner a salary, we are, once again back to the question of marginal rate planning.

Once we start looking at salaries above the level of the personal allowance, however, the issue is further complicated by the fact that the 'employer' partner's business will be liable for employer's secondary National Insurance Contributions on any additional salary at the rate of 12.8%.

But, the employer's National Insurance Contribution's themselves are allowable business deductions in their own right.

Hence, the additional cost of the secondary National Insurance Contributions to the employer partner's business is not usually the full 12.8%, but is usually lower due to the tax relief given on these contributions.

So, it all gets very messy!

It is also dependent on the *type* of business which the 'employer' partner has, so we will have to leave this subject here and return to it under the relevant sections later.

3.4   SOLE TRADERS PAYING SALARIES

As we know a very simple way for a self-employed sole trader partner to move income across to the other partner is to pay them a salary.

Where one partner is a self-employed sole trader, their business profits are taxed at rates from 0% up to 41%, as shown in section 2.5.

However, their *marginal* rate of tax may be something quite different and it is this rate, as well as their partner's marginal rate of tax, which is the key to any tax planning strategy.

There simply isn't enough space here to provide you with the optimum solution in every possible scenario. What I will do is look at the most simple scenario.

Where a sole trader partner has substantial business profits, well in excess of £37,295 (where higher rate tax kicks in), their marginal rate of tax will be 41%. Any payment of salary to their partner will therefore save the sole trader Income Tax and National Insurance at the combined rate of 41%.

However, as we saw in the previous section, once a salary of more than the current personal allowance is paid, we have to also start considering employer's secondary National Insurance Contribution's, payable at the rate of 12.8%.

So, concentrating just on the sole trader partner for the moment, the payment of salary above the personal allowance still continues to save them tax at the rate of 41% but at a cost of 12.8%. The National Insurance Contributions themselves, though, attract tax relief at a rate of 41%, so where does that leave us?

Example

Jessica has a very successful business as a self-employed freelance caterer and makes annual profits of over £40,000.

She employs her partner Jack in her business to help her clean tables and to provide her with a few other services.

Jessica already pays Jack more than the personal allowance but decides to give him a pay rise of £1,000.

This will cost her £128 in additional secondary National Insurance Contributions. However, all of her total additional cost of £1,128 is tax deductible and therefore saves £462.48 (i.e. 41%) tax and national insurance.

Jessica's net saving is therefore £334.48 (£462.48 - £128.00).

As we can see from the above example, the marginal rate tax saving for a high income sole trader paying additional salary to their partner over and above the personal allowance is 33%.

This net saving remains greater than the Income Tax and National Insurance paid by the employee partner on the salary as long as their total annual income does not exceed £37,295.

Subject to the possibility of more complex marginal rate considerations, therefore (including the case where the 'employee' partner has capital gains above the annual exemption), the simple rule of thumb is as follows:

Tax Tip

A payment of salary from a taxpayer with self-employment income falling into the higher rate tax band to a partner with total income below the higher rate threshold will usually save tax.

In the simplest case the maximum annual saving achievable for a couple simply by payment of a salary out of one partner's sole trader business income is as follows:

£4,895	@	41%	(	41%	-	0%	)	=	£2,006.95
£2,090	@	12.448%	(	33.448%	-	21%	)	=	£260.16
£25,775	@	0.448%	(	33.448%	-	33%	)	=	£115.47
£4,535	@	10.448%	(	33.448%	-	23%	)	=	£473.82
							Total	£2,856.40

Sole Traders with Lower Profits

When the sole trader partner's profits are below £37,295, the payment to their partner of any salary in excess of the personal allowance is very seldom worthwhile.

3.5 OTHER TAX SAVING IDEAS FOR SOLE TRADERS

Other tax deductible payments which a sole trader might make to a partner might include:

- Rent, where the partner owns the sole trader's business premises.
- Interest on loans from the other partner.

These types of payment are not subject to any National Insurance liabilities and are therefore generally more tax efficient than salary payments when they can be justified.

As with salaries, however, the payment must be made for the benefit of the trade or business and hence should never be at more than a normal, commercial rate.

Furthermore, in the case of loans, there will genuinely need to have been a loan made from the partner for business purposes. This will need to be structured carefully, with a proper loan agreement.

3.6 TAKING YOUR PARTNER INTO PARTNERSHIP

I told you that some of the terminology would get confusing!

What I'm talking about here is the idea of taking your relationship partner into partnership as your business partner. This is another useful way for a sole trader to 'share' their business income with their partner.

This has some very important non-tax implications which are covered in Chapter 12. As a consequence of these non-tax issues, it will often be wise to form a Limited Liability Partnership rather than a normal, common law, business partnership.

Furthermore, your partner will, of course, then own a share of your business. As with all other asset transfers, in order for the tax planning to be effective, your partner will need to have beneficial ownership of their share of the business and this means that they will have a great many rights over *your* business.

Leaving these issues aside for the moment, the main tax advantage of forming a business partnership with your partner instead of simply employing them is that you will not be liable for any employer's National Insurance Contributions on their earnings.

Furthermore, your partner will pay National Insurance on their profit share at the self-employed rate of 8%, rather than the employee rate of 11%.

So, as far as Income Tax and National Insurance are concerned, this is generally a more efficient tax saving strategy than employing your partner.

Example

By March 2005, Jessica's annual profits have reached £80,000 before accounting for her partner Jack's salary.

After several pay rises, Jack's salary has now reached £37,295 and, looking forward to 2005/2006, Jessica begins to wonder if she might be better off making him her business partner instead.

With Jack as an employee, Jessica's own tax liability for the year would work out as follows:

Profit for the year before Jack's salary				£80,000
Less:				
Jack's salary				£37,295
Employer's National Insurance @12.8%				£4,147

Jessica's net profit for the year				£38,558
Less: personal allowance				£4,895

				£33,663

Income Tax @	10%	on	£2,090	£209.00
Income Tax @	22%	on	£30,310	£6,668.20
Income Tax @	40%	on	£1,263	£505.20
National Insurance @	8%	on	£27,865	£2,229.20
National Insurance @	1%	on	£5,798	£57.98
Total				£9,669.58

Meanwhile, Jack would be paying £9,987.70 in Income Tax and National Insurance under the PAYE system.

The couple's total tax burden for the year would thus be **£23,804.28** [£9,669.58 + £9,987.70 + employer's national insurance of £4,147.00].

If Jack were an equal partner in the business, Jessica and he would both have the same tax liability for the year, as follows:

Partner profit share for the year	£40,000
Less: personal allowance	£4,895

	£35,105

Income Tax @	*10%*	*on £2,090*	*£209.00*
Income Tax @	*22%*	*on £30,310*	*£6,668.20*
Income Tax @	*40%*	*on £2,705*	*£1,082.00*
National Insurance @	*8%*	*on £27,865*	*£2,229.20*
National Insurance @	*1%*	*on £7,240*	*£72.40*
Total			*£10,260.80*

Multiply by two and you get the couple's total tax liability for the year: £20,521.60.

The couple could therefore save £3,282.68 if Jessica made Jack her business partner.

This is a pretty good saving. However, what Jessica will be asking herself is, can she trust Jack?

Aside from the issue of trust we also have to be wary of the possible impact of the settlements legislation when taking a partner into a business partnership.

The safest method is generally for them to be a business partner right from the outset. To date, Revenue & Customs has not sought to challenge this type of arrangement.

For an *existing* business, there are two basic methods to justify bringing your partner into a business partnership:

- The partner can buy their share of the business partnership, or
- The partner's profit share is justified by the amount of work that they do in the business.

The first method may have both Capital Gains Tax and Stamp Duty Land Tax implications. As usual, the Capital Gains Tax position will depend on your marital status. Stamp Duty Land Tax may sometimes arise where the business owns any land and buildings.

Whether you can use the second method will frequently depend on the type of business involved. For some types of business, such as lawyers, chartered accountants, doctors, etc, the rules of that particular profession would prevent you from bringing an unqualified partner into a business partnership.

Simply giving your partner a partnership share in your business, without them doing the necessary work to justify it, is probably going to fall foul of the settlements legislation in most cases, although there are some important exemptions which may sometimes apply for married couples and registered civil partners.

Partnership Agreement

When taking a partner into a business partnership, a well drafted partnership agreement is strongly recommended as a means of recording and formalising your new business relationship.

Capital Gains

Passing a business partnership share to your partner will affect your future Capital Gains Tax position on a sale of the business. The tax planning principles involved were considered in Chapter 2.

A share in a trading partnership will usually be a business asset for Capital Gains Tax taper relief purposes.

3.7   BUSINESS PARTNERSHIPS WITH THIRD PARTIES

The next situation which we need to consider is the case where one of the partners has a business partnership with someone else (i.e. not with their relationship partner).

The tax considerations here are really exactly the same as for a sole trader. They are, however, complicated by the fact that other people are also involved.

Your other business partners are therefore unlikely to want you to pay your partner a salary other than within the normal pay scale, as this will affect their profit shares.

If the same levels of salary are also paid to *their* relationship partners, however, they may become more amenable to the idea.

Payments such as rent or interest always need to be commercially justified in any case, so one would generally expect business partners to accept these where appropriate.

As for taking your partner into the business partnership, your existing business partners may be prepared to accept this if your partner's profit share effectively comes out of your own.

Example

Mickey, Donald and Goofy are in business together with equal shares.

Mickey and Donald each wish to bring their wives into the business. Goofy, however, is a single man and does not wish to reduce his profit share.

Mickey and Donald can achieve their objective whilst still protecting Goofy's position if they all agree to share profits as follows:

Mickey, Minnie, Donald & Daisy: One Sixth Each
Goofy: One Third

3.8   PRIVATE COMPANIES & COUPLES

When we come to couples where one or both partners have their own private company, our range of choices expands considerably.

The options to put salary, rent or interest income into our partner's hands all remain. One important difference is the marginal rate of tax saving involved as we now have to include the *company's* tax position.

In section 3.3 we discussed the application of the national minimum wage to our own partner. This remains equally true when we have our own company and can even further extend to ***ourselves!***

One useful exception to the application of the national minimum wage, however, is that it doesn't have to apply to the extent that a person's duties of employment in a private company consist of those of a director or company secretary. Beware though, this does not exempt *all* of such person's salary – it only applies to the hours spent on their duties as a director or company secretary.

Couples with their own private company have far greater scope to 'move' or 'convert' employment income. Furthermore, if it's your company then you can also count any saving in employer's National Insurance as your own.

Furthermore, putting shares in your own private company into your partner's hands provides the opportunity to 'move' another type of income: dividends.

3.9   PRIVATE COMPANY DIVIDENDS

We looked at the Income Tax saving potential of dividend income in section 2.12. Those principles will generally remain exactly the same in the case of your own private company paying dividends.

We do, however, need to be extra cautious with private company dividends when it comes to the settlements legislation. In terms of the settlements legislation the person trying to pass assets to a partner can be taxed on *all* the income.

In the case of private companies, we also have the option to issue shares to our partner and, indeed, to issue shares of different classes.

As far as an issue of ordinary shares is concerned, the settlements legislation should not apply as long as we carefully observe the principles outlined in section 2.9.

However, if the company falls into what is known as an 'Arctic Systems' type situation, you have to be extremely careful. More about this in the next section.

Other classes of shares can, however, give rise to problems whereby the settlements legislation is invoked and the relevant dividends are taxed on the wealthier partner.

These problems have mostly arisen as a result of attempts to get dividend income into a spouse's hands by the use of special classes of shares (often termed 'preference shares') which do not carry any other significant rights over the company. Generally, such shares would have no voting rights and only a very small, fixed, nominal capital value.

Revenue & Customs' viewpoint is that such shares are no more than an artificial mechanism to divert income and they will therefore attempt to overturn this type of arrangement whenever they can.

As far as I am aware, however, the settlements legislation has, to date, only been applied in this particular way in the case of *married* couples.

At present, therefore, it would seem that an unmarried couple may still be able to utilise special classes of shares to move dividend income into the hands of a partner with a lower tax rate without giving them any significant rights over the company. This legislation is very wide-ranging though, so we may soon see a similar attack on unmarried couples with private companies.

3.10 THE IMPLICATIONS OF 'ARCTIC SYSTEMS'

In the recent and now infamous tax case of 'Arctic Systems', Revenue & Customs successfully applied the principle that, by not taking a full commercial rate of salary out of the company, a taxpayer was making a settlement in favour of his partner who held shares in the company.

This case involved a married couple, Mr and Mrs Jones, who held perfectly normal ordinary shares in their own company. However, because Mr Jones performed all the work which gave the company its profits, but did not receive a commercial rate of salary for that work, Revenue & Customs invoked the settlement legislation and deemed all of the dividend income to belong to him.

The result of this decision was that Mr Jones had to pay Income Tax on dividends which should have been received tax free by Mrs Jones.

What's more, Mrs Jones actually did work in the business, just not enough to keep Revenue & Customs happy.

The result of the 'Arctic Systems' case has caused uproar in the tax world and the case has now gone to the Court of Appeal. At the time of writing, however, we are still awaiting the outcome of this appeal.

At present, it is hard to be sure how far this decision will spread. 'Arctic Systems' was a 'personal service company' whose profits were entirely derived from Mr Jones' own professional services, so the decision should not be generally applicable to all private companies owned by couples.

Furthermore, many commentators seem to be suggesting that this ruling will only apply where the shareholders are married couples or registered civil partnerships. I must say, however, that my own reading of the relevant legislation leaves me far from certain on this point.

Certainly, we can now expect Revenue & Customs to try to apply the same principles to any husband and wife companies where the profits are mainly derived from the professional activities of one spouse only.

Personally, I would tend to think that most trading companies, which carry a far higher degree of commercial risk than a personal service company, should be reasonably safe from an attack under 'Arctic Systems' principles.

Furthermore, the degree of danger of an attack must surely also depend on how much your partner is involved in the company's business. From now on, it would be wise to ensure that they are very actively involved.

3.11 PROPERTY BUSINESSES

Those with property businesses have a number of options available to share their income with their partners.

As usual, the benefit of each of these options needs to be assessed under the marginal rate principles which we covered in Chapter 2.

For starters a salary can be paid to your partner, if justified (see section 3.3). Remember though, that your own effective tax savings will be based on the marginal rates applying to rental income, not those applying to self-employment income.

Interest at commercial rates may be paid to your partner if they lend you money for the purpose of your property business. Again, a proper loan agreement is advisable.

In some cases, your partner could set up their own business providing property management services. The fees which you pay to them would then be a deductible cost against your own rental income. As usual, such fees must not exceed a commercial rate for the services provided. Your partner could even set up a property management services company for this purpose.

The possible benefits of sharing the rental income itself were covered in section 2.14. How you achieve this, however, is dependent on your *marital status*, so we will return to this subject in later chapters.

3.12   VAT

Lastly, before we leave the subject of couples in business, a couple of quick points on VAT for couples in business.

Firstly, if you have a VAT registered business, you must continue to charge VAT on any goods or services supplied to your partner. There are no special exemptions for partners, regardless of marital status.

If you and your partner are each in business, you may be able to separate your businesses so that each one has a turnover of less than the VAT registration limit (£60,000). You will therefore be able to avoid charging your customers VAT and yet perhaps have a combined turnover between you of anything up to £120,000.

Note, however, that to 'separate' your businesses for VAT purposes, each business must operate quite independently of the other and any goods or services supplied from the one business to the other must be accounted for very strictly.

Chapter 4

Unmarried Couples

4.1 WHAT IS AN 'UNMARRIED COUPLE'?

Before we plunge into looking at the tax consequences of being an 'unmarried couple', we'd better just establish very quickly what we mean by this term.

As far as this guide is concerned, an unmarried couple is made up of two adults in a long-term personal relationship who are neither married nor in a registered civil partnership.

As for what constitutes being married or in a registered civil partnership, I shall leave that to the next Chapter.

4.2 WHAT DIFFERENCE DOES IT MAKE?

The major differences to be aware of are as follows:

- There are no exemptions for transfers of assets between partners for either Capital Gains Tax or Inheritance Tax purposes.

- An unmarried couple are not deemed to be 'connected' for tax purposes (the significance of this is covered in section 5.8).

- Each member of an unmarried couple may have their own tax-exempt principal private residence for Capital Gains Tax purposes.

The most important of these is the first one. The Inheritance Tax consequences of remaining 'unmarried' will be covered in Chapter 10, so we will kick off this chapter by looking at Capital Gains Tax.

4.3 ASSET TRANSFERS FOR UNMARRIED COUPLES

As already stated, an unmarried couple are not generally 'connected' persons for tax purposes.

This is good, because being connected carries with it a lot of disadvantages. One of these is that a transfer of assets between connected persons, including a gift, is always deemed to take place at market value, often resulting in substantial Capital Gains Tax.

So, can an unmarried couple transfer assets between themselves at any price they like?

Sorry, no. At least not for Capital Gains Tax purposes anyway.

This is because another rule states that a transfer will also be deemed to take place at market value when one of the parties to the transaction does not intend to get the best deal for themselves out of the transaction.

In other words, if you give an asset to your partner, or try to sell it to them at a clearly absurd value, you will still end up being taxed as if you had sold it to them for its full market value.

In most cases, therefore, the fact that you are not 'connected' is actually of no real help when transferring assets to your partner. You are generally still forced to use market value.

Tax-free transfers can still be made by making use of the annual Capital Gains Tax exemption, taper relief and any available capital losses.

Furthermore, a property that used to be your main residence will generally be exempt from Capital Gains Tax if sold within three years of ceasing to be your home. A transfer of such a property to your partner should usually therefore be free from Capital Gains Tax.

Once we have exhausted these options however, we are left with only two other ways to get assets to our partner without incurring a Capital Gains Tax bill:

- Gifts of business assets – also known as hold over relief

- Transfers into a discretionary trust

4.4   BUSINESS ASSET TRANSFERS

Where the asset being transferred qualifies as a *business asset*, you and your partner can elect to 'hold over' the capital gain arising. In this way tax can be avoided.

Your partner will be treated as having bought it from you at the same price you paid for it.

You will be treated as having sold it at the price you paid for it so there will be no capital gain and no tax.

Example

Boris gives 10,000 shares in his private trading company, Karloff Ltd, to his partner Fay. The shares are now worth £75,000 but Boris and Fay make a joint election to 'hold over' the resulting capital gain.

Boris purchased the shares in 1999 at a price of £1 each, so Fay is now treated for Capital Gains Tax purposes as if she had bought the shares for £1 each – a total of £10,000.

Wealth Warning

Whilst the transferee is treated as having the same purchase cost as the transferor, they are not treated as having the same purchase *date*.

This means that it will take two years from the date of the transfer before the transferee is eligible for the maximum rate of taper relief on the transferred asset.

This could be disastrous if a sale of the asset takes place within this period.

Wealth Warning 2

Worse still, there could be some occasions when the transferor was eligible for business asset taper relief but the transferee is not!

Wealth Warning 3

The definition of business assets for the purpose of hold over relief is **not** the same as for taper relief.

Where the transferor acquired the asset before April 1998, they will be entitled to some indexation relief. This relief is given as a percentage of the cost of the asset, based on the date of purchase. The appropriate rates are given in Appendix D.

When the gain on such an asset is 'held over', the available indexation relief is transferred to the transferee.

Example

If Boris had, instead, bought his shares in July 1984, he would have been entitled to indexation relief of £8,250 (£10,000 x 82.5%).

Fay will still be treated as having acquired the shares for £10,000, but will also be able to claim the same £8,250 of indexation relief if she disposes of the Karloff Ltd shares.

Strictly, hold over relief is given for 'gifts' of business assets. This does not mean that it must be an outright gift, but there must be some element of gift.

If the transferor partner actually sells the asset to the transferee for any sum below the asset's full market value, they may still jointly elect to hold over the element of capital gain which exceeds the price actually paid.

Hence, if Boris had sold his shares to Fay for £40,000, they can elect to 'hold over' the £35,000 difference between this price and the shares' market value of £75,000.

Boris would then pay Capital Gains Tax on the basis of having sold the shares for £40,000 and Fay would be treated as having bought them for this price.

So, in a very round about way, we come to a position where an unmarried couple can choose the price at which assets are transferred. We are, however, limited to business assets only and the range of possible prices is also slightly limited.

They cannot create capital losses and they cannot make transfers at a price in excess of the asset's market value, but what unmarried couples can do is avoid Capital Gains Tax on business asset transfers or choose what level of Capital Gains Tax falling within these parameters they wish to pay.

Before we move on to some of the tax planning opportunities which this opens up, we need to define what exactly qualifies as a business asset for hold over relief purposes.

Business Assets for Hold Over Relief Purposes

The definition of business assets qualifying for this relief is much more restricted than the business asset definition for taper relief purposes as detailed in Appendix E.

The following items are qualifying business assets for hold over relief purposes:

- Assets used for the purposes of a trade carried on by the transferor or his personal company

- Property used by the transferor in a qualifying furnished holiday letting business in the UK

- Shares in an unquoted trading company, or

- Shares in the transferor's personal company

Broadly speaking, a 'personal company' means a trading company in which the transferor has at least 5% of the voting rights as a shareholder.

The holding company of a trading group also counts as a trading company for these purposes.

The qualification criteria for furnished holiday lettings can be found in the Taxcafe.co.uk guide *How To Avoid Property Tax'*.

Wealth Warning

Apart from qualifying furnished holiday letting businesses, buy-to-let properties are *not* business assets for the purposes of hold over relief.

4.5   INCREASE YOUR ALLOWABLE COSTS

The ability to 'name your price' by means of hold over relief on business assets can be used both to preserve indexation relief and to carry out a bit of 'bed and breakfasting' (see section 2.22).

This will enable an unmarried couple to both maximise allowable capital losses and minimise subsequent capital gains.

In some cases, this method could be used to effectively add four times the personal allowance on to the allowable cost of qualifying business assets every two years.

A few words of caution though:

- Each time a transfer takes place, the taper relief period has to start again and it will take two years to fully regain it.

- Both partners must be eligible for both business asset taper relief and hold over relief on the same assets if this strategy is to work.

- Each transfer will have a Stamp Duty cost @ 0.5% of the actual sale price where shares are concerned. In the case of land and buildings, the potential Stamp Duty Land Tax costs are more significant and will generally mean that this method is not cost effective.

- Transfers at less than market value may also have Inheritance Tax consequences, although shares in an unquoted trading company should be exempt.

As a consequence of these factors, I would generally only tend to suggest using the strategy of making repeated transfers under hold over relief for unquoted trading company shares.

4.6   USING DISCRETIONARY TRUSTS

If the asset which you wish to transfer to your partner would give you a Capital Gains Tax liability if sold at market value, and doesn't qualify as a business asset for hold over relief purposes, then the only method remaining to get income from that asset into your partner's hands without giving yourself a Capital Gains Tax bill is to use a discretionary trust.

Transfers into a discretionary trust fall into the Inheritance Tax system but allow you to escape Capital Gains Tax. You are allowed to hold over any capital gain when you transfer an asset to such a trust. This time, only the person making the transfer needs to make the election.

Transfers into a discretionary trust are what's known as 'chargeable transfers' for Inheritance Tax. Despite this you won't actually have to pay any Inheritance Tax as long as you don't make transfers with a total value of more than the nil rate band within a seven year period. The nil rate band currently stands at £275,000.

To use this method, it is absolutely essential that you do not benefit in any way from the assets held by the discretionary trust. Your spouse or registered civil partner is also not allowed to benefit, but that doesn't affect *unmarried* couples.

For the trust to be discretionary in nature, as required, there will have to be other beneficiaries in addition to your partner. Children always come in handy for this purpose, although you do have to avoid paying income from the trust to your own minor children, as this also messes things up.

Subject to this, you can then arrange for the trust to pay over the income from the transferred assets to your partner, who is the main beneficiary of the trust (if you wish).

The trust generally has to pay tax on all of its income as if it were a higher rate taxpayer. Beneficiaries who are not themselves higher rate taxpayers can, however, reclaim some of the tax paid where it exceeds the tax which they would have paid if they had received it directly. This is a complex matter, however, and it does not always result in all of this excess tax being reclaimed.

The assets do not have to stay in the trust forever, and could be transferred from the trust to your partner a few years later. A hold over claim can again be made at this point.

4.7   CRYSTALLISING GAINS

As explained in section 2.21, there are some occasions when it will be advantageous to create a capital gain now before changes in circumstances result in a loss of some time-sensitive relief.

We have already seen how this works for 'bed and breakfasting' where a transfer from one partner to the other can crystallise capital gains to utilise annual exemptions and capital losses brought forward and put them to their best effect.

For unmarried partners, unlike married couples or registered civil partners, a direct transfer from one to the other is sufficient to crystallise a capital gain for these purposes.

In this section, however, I will show you another couple of instances where crystallising a capital gain may be beneficial.

Disappearing Taper Relief

When a large capital gain has already accumulated on an asset qualifying for business asset taper relief, it may be better to crystallise the gain now rather then risk losing the benefit of this relief.

Example

Mac has some shares in The Village plc, a large quoted company. Mac bought the shares in January 2003 for £10,000 and has worked for The Village plc ever since.

By January 2006, Mac's shares are worth £80,000. However, he has just found a better job and intends to leave The Village plc's employment shortly.

Mac does not want to part with his shares yet but realises that as soon as he leaves his job they will cease to qualify for the generous 75% business asset taper relief (remember company employees who buy shares generally qualify for this type of taper relief).

Mac therefore decides to sell his shares to his partner Pat now in order to crystallise his capital gain while he still has an effective rate of only 10%.

Mac's Capital Gains Tax liability on these shares is as follows:

Sale proceeds:	*£80,000*
Less: Cost	*£10,000*

	£70,000
Taper relief @ 75%	*£52,500*

	£17,500
Annual exemption	*£8,500*

Taxable gain	*£9,000*
	=======

This gives Mac a Capital Gains Tax bill of £3,600.

Three years later, in January 2009, The Village plc is taken over by Big White Ball Inc and Pat receives sale proceeds of £100,000 for the shares.

118

Let's now compare Pat's Capital Gains Tax position with what Mac's would have been if he had still held the shares:

	Pat	**Mac**
Sale proceeds:	*£100,000*	*£100,000*
Less: Cost	*£80,000*	*£10,000*
	-------------	-------------
	£20,000	*£90,000*
Taper relief @ 75% for 'business asset' period = £90,000 x 3/6 x 75%	*n/a*	*£33,750*
Taper relief for remaining period @ 5%/20%	*£1,000*	*£9,000*
	-------------	-------------
	£19,000	*£47,250*
Annual exemption 2008/2009	*£9,400*	*£9,400*
	-------------	-------------
Taxable gain:	*£9,600*	*£37,850*
	=======	=======

The taxable gain in 2008/2009 has been reduced by £28,250 by selling the shares, saving £11,300 on that occasion, or a net £7,700 when we take Mac's earlier Capital Gains Tax liability into account.

There are some risks attached to this strategy and it may not always work out in your favour but in the right circumstances it is still well worth considering.

Former Homes

As we know from section 4.3, a former main residence will generally remain fully exempt from Capital Gains Tax for the first three years after it ceases to be the owner's home.

After that, the proportion of the overall gain which is exempt from Capital Gains Tax will usually reduce over time.

Crystallising a gain at an early enough stage by transferring the property to your partner should ensure that the accumulated capital gain up to that point will continue to be protected from Capital Gains Tax. It will also put the asset into your partner's hands which may be useful for marginal rate tax planning purposes.

Whether this is beneficial in the long run will depend on the relative future growth in value of the property when compared to the existing capital gain.

Example

Clint has a house which he bought in June 1998 and lived in as his main residence until June 2002. He knows that if he sells it by June 2005, his capital gain will be fully covered by the principal private residence exemption. He decides therefore to give the house to his partner Sondra.

The gift is free from Capital Gains Tax because, although it is deemed to take place at market value, Clint's principal private residence relief exempts him from any Capital Gains Tax liability.

Sondra sells the house in June 2012 and is fully taxable on the gain arising over the period since Clint transferred the property to her in 2005. [In reality, there are a number of reliefs which would come into play here, as detailed in the Taxcafe.co.uk guide How To Avoid Property Tax.*]*

120

In broad terms, however, subject to the various reliefs which Sondra might be able to claim, this strategy will be beneficial if the increase in value in the property from 1998 to 2005 is greater than the increase in value from 2005 to 2012.

In practice, it will be very difficult to be sure whether such a transfer would ultimately be beneficial. It's worth thinking about though.

Practical Pointer

If undertaking planning of this nature, it is important to be reasonably certain of the market value which will be applied to the property at the date of transfer from one partner to the other. This value will, of course, end up being the transferee partner's deductible cost at the time of the property's ultimate sale to a third party.

It is therefore wise to obtain a formal valuation from a professional valuer at the time of the transfer. Whilst Revenue & Customs might ultimately seek to substitute their own valuation, you would then have the appropriate evidence to support your valuation. At the very least, you will have a good idea of the approximate market value at the time of the transfer, even if Revenue & Customs should eventually succeed in applying a different value.

Wealth Warning

Market value will clearly apply in the case of an outright gift from one partner to the other. In the case of an actual sale, however, it is possible that the actual price paid might become the transferee partner's deductible cost if it is not too far away from the property's true open market value.

In a case like Clint and Sondra, for example, if Clint had sold the house to Sondra for a few thousand pounds less than its open market value, Revenue & Customs would probably argue that the actual price paid should form Sondra's deductible cost on the ultimate sale of the property.

Conversely, if they felt that Sondra had overpaid for the property, Revenue & Customs could insist on restricting Sondra's deductible cost to the property's market value at the time of the transfer.

Unfortunately, this is another case of 'Heads They Win, Tails You Lose' and it means that you need to pick your transfer value very carefully.

4.8 HOW TO HAVE TWO MAIN RESIDENCES

Whilst we're on the subject of main residences, it is worth looking at the potential tax benefits for unmarried couples of having two homes.

Each member of an unmarried couple may have their own qualifying main residence for Capital Gains Tax purposes. Between them, therefore, the couple have the potential to have two 'main residences', each of which will be exempt from Capital Gains Tax under the principal private residence exemption.

For those who regard themselves as a couple, and yet live apart, this is pretty simple to achieve since they each have their own home in any case.

Most unmarried couples, however, tend to live together and hence will often still have just one main residence as a couple, despite the fact that the tax legislation would allow them to have two.

In the typical situation, the unmarried couple will buy a property jointly together and occupy it as their main residence. Each partner will be exempt from Capital Gains Tax on their share of any capital gain when the property is sold.

In effect, each partner is managing to exempt half a property from Capital Gains Tax under the principal private residence exemption. Between them, they have exempted one property when they could exempt two. One principal private residence exemption is therefore wasted.

Naturally, if the couple can only afford to own one property this is not much of an issue. However, in many cases, they may also acquire a second property and this is where it becomes vital not to waste one of their principal private residence exemptions.

Main Residence Elections for Unmarried Couples

Whenever any individual has a legal or equitable interest in more than one private residential property which is their own home, they may elect which property should be regarded as their main residence for the purposes of the Capital Gains Tax principal private residence exemption.

A legal interest in a property means any form of ownership, sole or joint, including freehold, leasehold and the tenancy of a property rented under a lease. We will come back to the possible significance of the term 'equitable interest' later in this section.

Unlike married couples or registered civil partnerships, unmarried couples should not make joint main residence elections, but should each make their own separate elections in respect of their own shares in the relevant properties. Furthermore, unmarried couples do not need to both elect in favour of the same property at the same time and may each make elections in favour of different properties, where appropriate.

Each person has a deadline of two years from the date on which they first have a 'legal or equitable interest' in two or more private residences to make their election.

A main residence election must be made in writing, should be addressed to 'Her Majesty's Inspector of Taxes' and sent to your tax office in time to reach them before the second anniversary of the day on which you first had a legal or equitable interest in two or more private residences.

There is no particular prescribed form for the election, although the following example wording would be suitable for inclusion:

'In accordance with section 222(5) Taxation of Chargeable Gains Act 1992, I hereby nominate [Property] as my main residence with effect from [Date*].'

* - The first such election which you make will automatically be treated as coming into effect from the beginning of the period to which it relates. It is this first election to which the two year time limit applies.

However, once an election is in place, it may subsequently be changed, by a further written notice given to the Inspector under the same procedure, at any time. Such a new election may be given retrospective effect, if desired, by up to two years.

The reason changes to an existing main residence election are so useful revolves around the fact that the last three years of ownership of a former main residence are exempt from Capital Gains Tax.

We have already seen in previous sections that a former home usually remains fully exempt from Capital Gains Tax for three years after ceasing to be the owner's main residence.

However, this exemption actually extends somewhat further and the last three years of ownership of any property which has been your only or main residence *at any time* during your ownership will almost always be exempt from Capital Gains Tax.

So, yes, an unmarried couple can exempt some of the gain on a second home by making main residence elections. However, apart from achieving the exemption for the last three years of ownership on both properties, this will often still leave a large part of the gain on one property exposed to Capital Gains Tax.

However, if you can manage to have one main residence each, it would be possible to fully exempt both properties.

Let me explain the vital difference between these two approaches with a two-part example.

Example Part 1: 'How To Waste A principal private residence exemption'

Marion and John, an unmarried couple, bought a house in Manchester together in April 1998 as joint tenants.

In December 2005 they buy a holiday cottage in the Lake District, again as joint tenants. They use the cottage as a second home. On the advice of their accountant, they each make an election before December 2007 that the Manchester house should be regarded as their main residence for Capital Gains Tax purposes.

After spending two weeks in August 2011 staring at unrelenting rain through the windows of their Lake District cottage, Marion and John decide to sell it. When they return to Manchester in September, their accountant advises them to make new main residence elections in favour of the Lake District cottage. A week later, the accountant gets them to do a third pair of main residence elections, this time in favour of the Manchester house once more.

Marion and John's accountant explains that the two new sets of elections will ensure that the Lake District cottage is treated as each partner's main residence for one week during their ownership of it and that the last three years of each partner's ownership will therefore also be exempt from Capital Gains Tax. These three years of exemption are achieved at the cost of losing just one week's worth of exemption on their Manchester house.

In December 2011, Marion and John sell the Lake District cottage and realise a total capital gain of £200,000 (or £100,000 each). (It was a big cottage!)

Each partner has an identical Capital Gains Tax calculation, as follows:

Capital Gain (Each)		£100,000
Principal Private Residence Relief		
for 3 years out of 6		£50,000
		£50,000
Taper Relief @	20%	£10,000
		£40,000
Annual exemption for 2011/2012		£10,300
Taxable gain		£29,700

Marion and John's total Capital Gains Tax liability between them may therefore be as much as £23,760 (£29,700 x2 @ 40%).

As things stand, they are unlikely to have any Capital Gains Tax liability on a sale of their Manchester house, as the loss of just one week's principal private residence exemption will have only a negligible effect and any remaining taxable gain will probably be covered by their annual exemptions as long as they make no other capital gains in the same tax year as they sell the house.

Furthermore, if Marion and John sell the Manchester house within three years of the effective date of their second set of main residence elections made in September 2011, it will still be fully covered by their principal private residence exemptions.

Hence, Marion and John are probably pretty pleased with their accountant. But should they be?

Example Part 2: 'How To Have Two Main Residences'

Katie and Wayne are also unmarried and also live together in Manchester in a house which they bought together in April 1998 as joint tenants.

Katie and Wayne also decide to buy a cottage in the Lake District in December 2005.

However, Katie and Wayne's accountant gives two very different pieces of advice from Marion and John's accountant.

Firstly, he suggests that the Manchester house should be transferred into Katie's sole name. Wayne has therefore made a disposal of his share of the property which will be deemed to have taken place at market value. Wayne's capital gain is, however, fully covered by the principal private residence exemption, so that no Capital Gains Tax liability arises.

Secondly, the accountant advises Wayne to buy the Lake District cottage in his sole name. As this is now the only private residence which Wayne owns, it must be regarded as his main residence and any gain which he makes on the property will therefore be fully exempted under the principal private residence exemption.

Hence, when Wayne also sells his Lake District cottage in December 2011 (after an atrocious summer) and also makes a capital gain of £200,000, he will have no Capital Gains Tax to pay.

The second strategy adopted by Katie and Wayne would therefore appear to have saved the couple up to £23,760, as well as avoiding any possible (though probably minimal) exposure to Capital Gains Tax on their Manchester home.

So, what do we think of Marion and John's accountant now?

Furthermore, Katie and Wayne's saving compared to a couple who had undertaken no Capital Gains Tax planning at all and hence never made any of the appropriate main residence elections (nor ensured that their annual exemptions were available), could actually be up to £80,000!

The Equitable Interest Dilemma

As we saw in the previous example, once Wayne had divested himself of his ownership of one property, the other property automatically became his main residence for Capital Gains Tax purposes.

This arises as a result of a principle which is actually enshrined in Revenue & Customs' own manuals. Revenue & Customs' Capital Gains manual sets out the principle that where an individual's main home is occupied under licence, but they also own another residence, the residence which that individual owns is their only or main residence.

For this principle to work, however, we need to be sure of two things:

- The second home must be the taxpayer's private residence (we will return to this point shortly), and
- The main home must be occupied under licence.

To occupy a property under licence means that the taxpayer occupies the property despite having no legal or equitable interest in it.

A legal interest in the property includes all forms of ownership, right down to a short tenancy for a minimal weekly rent. In our example, we were able to ensure that Wayne had no legal interest in his Manchester home.

There is a dilemma, however, in the shape of a partner's possible equitable interest in the couple's main home.

If an individual stays rent free with family or friends, they are occupying the property under a gratuitous licence and there is clearly no equitable interest.

An unmarried partner in a co-habiting couple, however, has certain rights. These rights are further strengthened with effect from 5th December 2005 under the Civil Partnership Act and, in this regard, the Act applies equally to all unmarried couples.

The rights of an unmarried partner may therefore be sufficient to give them an equitable interest in the couple's main home. If so, the second home does not automatically become a partner's main residence simply because they divest themselves of any legal title to the main home.

But, on the other hand, a taxpayer may not make a main residence election unless he or she has a legal or equitable interest in two or more residences.

If we're uncertain as to whether an equitable interest exists in the main home, are we able to make an election in favour of the second home? That's the dilemma.

The Solution to the Dilemma

When you think about it though, the solution is simple:

Each partner should make a main residence election in favour of the property which they own.

In our example, Wayne should elect in favour of the Lake District cottage and Katie should elect in favour of the Manchester house. Both of them will need to elect by December 2007.

If each partner does have an equitable interest in the other's property then the elections will resolve the problem.

If no equitable interest exists then the elections are invalid. However, whilst the elections are invalid, it doesn't matter anyway, because each partner is automatically treated as having their main residence in the property which they own.

Establishing A Property As A Residence

The second point which we need to resolve is to ensure that the second home does become the private residence of the partner who owns it.

Whilst the main residence election can be used to ensure that one of a taxpayer's residences is treated as their main residence, it remains necessary to ensure that the property is their private residence in the first place.

To be a private residence, the taxpayer needs to make some private use of the property. Actual physical occupation of the property part of the time is essential for this purpose. Spending one weekend per month in the property, for example, should generally be sufficient for this purpose.

The taxpayer's private use of the property would need to continue for a reasonable period. What is 'reasonable' depends on the facts of the case. Generally, I would recommend at least two years, although, where circumstances do genuinely prevent this, a shorter period might sometimes be acceptable.

More often however, Revenue & Customs are concerned mainly with the 'quality' of the taxpayer's occupation of the property rather than the length of time involved. The taxpayer's 'quality' of occupation needs to be sufficient to be commensurate with that of a private residence. This, for example, would include furnishing the property to a sufficient standard to make it a comfortable home.

Subject to my further comments below, it is also important not to advertise the property for sale or rent until the 'reasonable' period discussed above has expired.

Once the property ceases to be used by the owner as a private residence, it will cease to be treated as their main residence for Capital Gains Tax purposes. Nevertheless, the principal private residence exemption will generally continue to cover the last three years of ownership of the property.

Renting Out Your Holiday Home

The property cannot be regarded as a private residence at any time when it is being used for some other purpose, including, in particular, when it is being rented out.

If you rent the property out under a formal lease, it will clearly cease to be your private residence immediately.

However, there remains the question of whether you can rent out your second home as holiday accommodation.

Here we come back to the issue of your 'quality' of occupation. If the property is rented out to such an extent that your own enjoyment of the property is hindered to the point where it can no longer be regarded as a 'home' then you will lose the benefit of private residence status on the property from that point onwards.

It is worth noting, however, that the tax advantages of a property which qualifies as 'furnished holiday accommodation' are significant (see the Taxcafe.co.uk guide *'How To Avoid Property Tax'* for details). It is highly unlikely that the same property could qualify as both furnished holiday accommodation and as the owner's principal private residence at the same time.

Where, however, the property is rented out to a far lesser extent, perhaps for the occasional use of family or friends, for example, then the principal private residence exemption may continue to apply.

If the tenants merely occupy the property under gratuitous licence, either rent-free, or by making a nominal contribution to running costs, this should not hinder the property's main residence status.

If there is some degree of profit involved in the renting out of the property, but it is not so great as to prevent the property from being regarded as the owner's home, then the principal private residence exemption will continue, but will be restricted by reference to the rental periods.

Tax Tip – Foreign Properties

A second home located abroad can be treated as one partner's main residence for Capital Gains Tax purposes under exactly the same principles as already outlined above.

Under the right circumstances, this provides scope to have a Capital Gains Tax-free foreign holiday home!

Do watch out for foreign taxes though!

Wealth Warning

Where an unmarried couple hold property for their own private residential use in a different proportion to the proportionate funds provided by each partner, there is a risk of Income Tax charges arising under the 'pre-owned asset regime'.

Such charges can easily be avoided by making the appropriate election, as detailed in section 4.11. This, in turn, may have adverse Inheritance Tax consequences however, as examined in Chapter 10.

4.9 JOINTLY HELD PROPERTIES

An unmarried couple owning a property jointly may split the income from that property in a different proportion to their actual ownership of the property.

I would recommend that there is some commercial rationale for the income split. For example, one partner may receive an increased share of the income because they are responsible for the maintenance of the property or for dealing with tenants.

A formal written agreement confirming the agreed income split is required.

Subject to the above comments, the rental income split may be altered from year to year, though not retrospectively.

It is essential that each partner does indeed receive their agreed share of the income. As discussed in section 2.10, it will therefore often be preferable not to pay the income into a joint bank account.

4.10 MULTIPLE COMPANIES

If two connected persons each control a company, this will often have a detrimental effect on those companies' Corporation Tax rates.

An unmarried couple, however, are not connected and can therefore run one company each without any adverse impact on their Corporation Tax bills.

In fact, to be precise, all that is required is for each of them to control one of the companies (i.e. be the majority shareholder). The other partner can be a minority shareholder in each case without damaging the Corporation Tax position.

4.11 PRE-OWNED ASSETS

As well as potential Inheritance Tax liabilities, a transfer of funds or assets from one unmarried partner to the other can potentially cause an Income Tax charge to arise under the 'pre-owned asset' regime.

This charge arises if the original transferor subsequently benefits from the transferred asset.

The charge also arises if the transferor benefits from assets purchased with transferred funds, or with the sale proceeds of an asset transferred previously.

This will often be a problem in the case of unmarried partners buying a home together.

Example

Chris and Ann are buying a house together. They need a deposit of £50,000. Ann has the money to hand but Chris doesn't have any savings. Ann therefore pays the whole deposit herself. They take out a mortgage in both names and buy the house as joint tenants. (Although it wouldn't make any difference here if they were tenants in common or the house was in Scotland.)

As soon as Ann moves into the house, she is benefiting from the effective transfer of £25,000 to Chris which arose when Ann paid the deposit on the house. This means that Ann is potentially subject to an Income Tax charge on the value of this 'benefit in kind'.

In innocent cases like this, there is a simple answer. The affected taxpayer (the original transferor) can simply elect to 'opt out' of the Income Tax charge by agreeing to include the transferred assets or funds in their own estate for Inheritance Tax purposes. This election needs to be made by 31st January following the end of the tax year in which the charge would have arisen.

Hence, in our example, if Ann had moved into the house during 2005/2006, she would need to make the election by 31st January 2007.

4.12   WHAT IF YOU CAN'T TRUST YOUR PARTNER

If you don't trust your partner, you need a trust!

A discretionary trust could be used for this purpose and has the added advantage of the availability of hold over relief, as discussed in section 4.6.

Alternatively, if you are only concerned with ensuring that your partner cannot run off with the assets which you wish them to get the income from, you could use a life interest trust. This type of trust is also sometimes referred to as an 'interest in possession trust'.

Under a life interest trust, your partner can get all the income but cannot get their hands on the assets themselves. Ultimately, on your partner's death, or at some other time, the assets can pass to someone else.

'Someone else' could be anyone but would typically be your children.

Most importantly, however, you yourself must not be able to benefit from the trust. If you do, then the settlements legislation would tax all of the trust's income as if it were yours.

Having said that, tax planning is not always the only motive present when these trusts are set up, so there will be cases where the transferor is willing to accept this tax burden in order to safeguard the assets.

There are no Capital Gains Tax exemptions available for transfers of assets into a life interest trust. If other exemptions apply, however, (e.g. principal private residence relief or hold over relief on gifts of business assets) then they will be unaffected by the fact that the transferee is a trust.

Chapter 5

Marriage and Civil Partnerships

5.1 FOR RICHER OR POORER

The concept of marriage has existed in most of the World's cultures for thousands of years. Traditionally, its primary purpose was for the security of women and children in eras long ago when a man's protection was seen as essential. Cultural and religious factors have also added to its importance throughout most of the World for many years.

In recent decades, however, the status of marriage as a cultural and social necessity has diminished somewhat and many people now choose to live as unmarried couples without fearing the cultural backlash that may have existed in times past.

The status of marriage has long been enshrined in UK law, including, most importantly from our point of view, tax law.

The married couple have had a unique and special tax status in UK tax law for centuries.

Despite changing times and a new social and cultural environment, that special status still continues to this day.

What the recent social changes do mean, however, is that marriage is now more of a personal choice than ever before. Without the cultural pressure to marry which used to exist, the relevance of taxation and other financial matters in making this decision becomes all the more important.

On 5th December 2005, a major change will take place in the UK. From that day onwards, same sex couples will be able to enter into registered civil partnerships, with all of the same rights, privileges and obligations as married couples.

The equality of rights for registered civil partnerships will extend into the realm of UK tax law. The special status of the married couple in UK tax will therefore cease to be unique, as registered civil partners will, from that day onwards, enjoy the same status.

Between the social changes of recent decades and the legal change set to take place on 5th December 2005, what this means is that everyone, regardless of their sexuality, will soon face the same choice, namely whether to 'tie the knot' in a legally binding sense and become a legal 'couple' or remain an independent individual for legal and tax purposes.

And that's where one of this guide's main objectives comes in. Because everyone has a choice and that choice may, to some extent be based on tax considerations, it's vital to understand what you are getting yourself into.

Remember, it isn't all good news. There are both advantages and disadvantages to the tax status of a married couple or civil partnership.

So, it really is a case of:

'for better or worse and for richer or poorer'!

5.2   WHAT IS A SPOUSE?

"What a daft question", you're probably thinking. Well it isn't – read on.

The main thing which it is essential to understand is that the special tax status afforded to a married couple only applies if they are legally married.

Some tax and related matters do apply to unmarried co-habiting couples but, by and large, the tax advantages of marriage do not generally apply to common-law spouses.

I tried to find a definition of marriage within the tax legislation, but it seems that marriage is one of those concepts which is regarded as so fundamental that there is no need to define it!

This is not terribly helpful. In fact, the only thing which is specified in Revenue & Customs' own manuals is that a marriage can only be recognised where it is between a person of male gender at birth and a person of female gender at birth.

Under UK law, a person's gender is fixed and determined at birth, although I understand that there are moves to allow gender reassignments to be given legal recognition.

5.3   SHAM MARRIAGES

In view of the tremendous advantages which marriage or civil partnership may sometimes confer for tax purposes, I began to wonder if the tax authorities had ever tried to overturn a marriage on the basis that it was a mere 'sham'.

Whilst such arguments are more commonly encountered by those dealing with the immigration authorities, a little research unearthed just such an attack by the Inland Revenue back in 1936.

Mr Dale, the intended victim of this attack, had married in 1921 and, under the rules prevailing at the time, had therefore claimed a higher personal allowance for income tax purposes. In 1933, however, Mr Dale's marriage was annulled – declared null and void by court decree. The Inland Revenue then attempted to assess additional Income Tax on Mr Dale by withdrawing the higher personal allowance which he had claimed for the period from 1921 to 1933.

The good news is that the court held that Mr Dale was entitled to the married man's allowance for the entire period between his marriage and its subsequent annulment. The Inland Revenue had no right to challenge his marital status during this period, even though the marriage was eventually declared null and void.

Hence, it would appear that there is currently no legal basis for Revenue & Customs to challenge the validity of a marriage.

5.4   WHAT IS A CIVIL PARTNER?

It seems reasonable to expect that the same principles as outlined in section 5.2 will be applied as far as possible.

Hence, the civil partnership will not generally be effective for tax purposes unless formally registered.

5.5   SHAM CIVIL PARTNERSHIPS

Again, we must consider the possibility that Revenue & Customs might, in future, challenge the validity of a registered civil partnership.

My fear is that, as a new institution, civil partnership will, at least initially, be less well respected and that the danger of such a challenge will therefore be much greater.

However, Revenue & Customs are bound by the Taxpayer's Charter to treat all taxpayers equally and this should be used to counter any such challenges where there appears to be any undue prejudice. If there are no legal grounds for them to challenge the validity of marriages, it would be unfair if they were to attempt to mount any challenges against registered civil partnerships.

5.6   OVERSEAS MARRIAGES AND CIVIL PARTNERSHIPS

Overseas Marriages

Generally speaking, a couple who are legally married under the laws of another country will similarly be recognised as legally married for all legal purposes in the UK. Naturally, this includes UK taxation law.

This is enshrined in a written Parliamentary answer from 1978 in Hansard which states:

"For Income Tax purposes, a marriage is accepted as valid if it is valid under the law of the country in which it was performed and of the country of domicile of the parties."

Domicile is a taxation concept broadly similar to nationality and is a subject which we will return to later, in section 11.3.

What the Hansard statement means therefore is that foreign nationals who marry abroad, in their own country, should be accepted as being legally married for UK tax purposes.

However, it also follows that both UK and foreign nationals who marry abroad, outside their own country, need to take care that their marriage will be recognised for UK tax purposes.

The greatest difficulties arise in the case of polygamous marriages recognised under the laws of another country. Revenue & Customs' view on these, for Income Tax purposes at least, can be found in section 9.5.

Overseas Civil Partnerships

Civil partnerships are now recognised in nine member states of the European Union, as well as New Zealand, Iceland and some parts of Canada and the USA.

The legal status of a registered civil partnership under the law of another country should be recognised as having legal effect in the UK from 5th December 2005 (although, at the time of writing, this is not absolutely certain and it may be a little later).

This legal recognition will be of enormous importance to those couples in a civil partnership which has been legally registered abroad. In effect, their marital status for UK tax purposes will change on the date that this legal recognition comes into force, just as if they had entered a UK registered civil partnership on that day. It is very important for couples in this position to be aware of this.

5.7   ADVANTAGE OR DISADVANTAGE?

Throughout these sections, I will be referring to the tax advantages and tax disadvantages of marriage and registered civil partnerships.

Where some aspect of the tax system is predominantly advantageous to married couples and registered civil partners, I will naturally refer to this as a tax advantage. Similarly, anything which is predominantly disadvantageous will be referred to as a tax disadvantage.

However, it is essential to bear in mind that almost every tax advantage can sometimes prove disadvantageous if you are unfortunate enough to be caught on the wrong side of the rules. Consider this, for example:

Example

Liz has some private company shares which will realise a capital gain of £8,500 if she sells them. She wants to keep control of this shareholding, but also wants to utilise her annual Capital Gains Tax exemption (which, coincidentally, happens to be £8,500 for 2005/2006).

Liz hits on the idea of selling her shares to her husband Richard – that way, she figures, she will keep the shares 'in the family' but also utilise her annual Capital Gains Tax exemption.

Sadly, Liz's plan is fundamentally flawed. The sale of shares to Richard will be deemed to be a 'no gain no loss' transaction for Capital Gains Tax purposes. Most of the time this would be regarded as a tax advantage, as it provides all married couples and registered civil partners with the opportunity to transfer assets between each other free from any taxation. However, in Liz's case, this concession undoes her little tax planning scheme and leaves her Capital Gains Tax exemption wasted.

What this example illustrates, however, is the fact that, when it comes to marriage or civil partnership and tax reliefs, one man's meat is very much another man's poison.

Thankfully, the opposite position is equally true – namely that many so-called tax disadvantages can often be turned to advantage with careful planning. We have already seen many examples of this in Chapter 4.

5.8   CONNECTED PERSONS

The tax authorities have long since recognised that certain people are likely to collaborate with each other to reduce their overall tax burden. They call this tax avoidance, I call it tax planning.

The term used to describe these likely collaborators is 'connected persons'.

In essence, there is a basic presumption in the tax legislation that connected persons do not deal with each other on normal commercial, 'arms' length' terms. The onus is therefore on the taxpayer to prove otherwise.

On the other hand, where two parties to a transaction are not connected the onus of proof that there is a tax avoidance motive is on Revenue & Customs.

Hence, one can readily see that where two parties are connected for tax purposes, the degree of difficulty in carrying out effective tax planning will increase.

Connected persons include your mother, your father, your son, your daughter, etc, etc, (see Appendix C for a full list).

Most importantly though, for the purposes of this guide, your husband, wife or registered civil partner is a connected person for tax purposes.

Conversely, a common-law spouse, unregistered same sex partner or any other non-legally registered co-habitee is not a connected person. This could even include the other parent of your children!

Whilst each parent is connected with their children for tax purposes, the parents are not connected with each other if they are not legally married or in a registered civil partnership.

Hence, quite simply, when you get married or enter a registered civil partnership, you become connected with your spouse or partner for tax purposes. You are thus effectively volunteering to be subject to reams and reams of tax legislation aimed at preventing tax avoidance; legislation which would not apply if you were not legally married or in a registered civil partnership.

This connected status lies at the heart of most of the tax disadvantages arising from marriage or civil partnership.

5.9   THE MAJOR BENEFIT OF MARRIAGE OR CIVIL PARTNERSHIP

Asset Transfers

Perhaps the most significant taxation benefit of marriage or registered civil partnerships is the ability for most couples to transfer assets to each other free from taxation.

Whilst married couples and registered civil partners are connected persons for tax purposes, the transfer of any asset from one member of the couple or partnership to the other is completely exempt from Capital Gains Tax.

Secondly, where the transferee is UK domiciled (see section 11.3) the transfer of assets to a spouse or registered civil partner is also exempt from Inheritance Tax and also specifically exempted from any charges under the pre-owned assets regime (see section 4.11).

5.10   THE MAJOR PITFALLS OF MARRIAGE OR CIVIL PARTNERSHIP

Private Residences

One of the biggest disadvantages of marriage or registered civil partnership is the fact that the couple will lose a principal private residence.

A 'principal private residence' means, quite simply, your home. If you have more than one private residence, it is generally your main home.

Every single adult person, who is neither married nor in a registered civil partnership, can have their own principal private residence which is exempt from Capital Gains Tax.

However, once you marry or enter a registered civil partnership, you can only have one Capital Gains Tax exempt principal private residence between you.

Hence, a couple who had one principal private residence each before they 'tie the knot' will lose the Capital Gains Tax exempt status on one of them.

We will return to this subject in detail in section 6.4.

Settlements

Another major disadvantage of marriage or registered civil partnership is the fact that the settlements legislation (see section 2.9) is extended to any 'settlements' where you may still benefit from the assets you have transferred.

There is an exemption to this rule in the case of an *outright* gift to your spouse or registered civil partner. This exemption enables us to still do most of our marginal rate tax planning via transfers of assets to a spouse or registered civil partner.

The exemption does not apply in the case of a gift of an asset which is merely 'wholly or mainly a right to income'. This is why some of the preference share type schemes discussed in section 3.9 do not work in practice.

The extension of the settlements legislation to income flowing to a spouse or registered civil partner from assets which are not outright gifts means that we cannot use trusts to get income into the hands of a spouse or registered civil partner for tax purposes without entrusting them with the underlying asset.

Well, not usually anyway – see section 7.5.

5.11   WHERE IT DOESN'T MATTER

Whilst this chapter is mainly concerned with changes in your tax situation which arise on marriage or registration of a civil partnership, I will just spend a little time briefly summarizing the main areas of taxation which are *unaffected* by the change in your legal status.

It may also serve to dispel a few myths!

Tax Credits

Any co-habiting heterosexual couple must make any claim for Child Tax Credits or Working Tax Credits on a joint basis whether they are legally married or not.

From 5th December 2005, the same will be true for co-habiting same sex couples whether they register as a civil partnership or not!

Employing Your Partner

As we saw in Chapter 3, many people with their own business put their partner on the payroll and pay them a modest salary, often in line with the personal allowance.

If you employ your partner you must operate PAYE and deduct and account for National Insurance Contributions in exactly the same way as for any other employee. Whether you subsequently marry or enter a registered civil partnership makes absolutely no difference to your obligations as an employer.

Stamp Duty, Stamp Duty Land Tax and VAT

There are no exemptions for any of these so-called 'indirect' taxes when the parties to the transaction are married or registered civil partners.

Chapter 6

Tax Planning on Marriage or Registration

6.1 A LEGAL METAMORPHOSIS

Most people probably give it very little thought, but the moment that you say "I do", you will completely change your tax status.

For many UK tax purposes, you cease to be an individual and become part of a couple who are inextricably linked together.

As of 5th December 2005, the same is true for civil partners at the moment of registration and, as I mentioned in section 5.6, some couples who have already registered their civil partnership overseas will also undergo this metamorphosis on the date that the UK legislation chooses to recognise them.

On your wedding day, registration day or date of legal recognition, a number of key changes to your tax situation will take place:

- The complete Capital Gains Tax exemption for transfers of assets to your spouse or registered civil partner comes into force.
- The Inheritance Tax exemption for transfers of assets to your spouse or registered civil partner comes into force.
- You will only be permitted to have one principal private residence between you.
- You become 'connected persons' for all tax purposes.
- If one or both of you were born before 6th April 1935, you will become entitled to the married couples allowance.

6.2   ACTION BEFORE MARRIAGE OR REGISTRATION

Before you get married or register your civil partnership, it makes sense to 'take stock' of your tax situation and see if there is anything useful you can do whilst you and your partner are still separate persons for tax purposes.

What I'd suggest here is that you take a look at Chapter 4 and consider whether any of the tax planning measures there, which apply only to unmarried couples, could be of benefit to you. If so, you need to carry them out before your wedding or registration day.

If you wish to crystallise a capital gain, for example, and plan to do this by transferring the asset to your partner, you should make sure that the transfer takes place before your wedding or registration day.

You may also need to revisit some of the tax planning which you carried out previously.

If each of you controls your own private company, for example, (see section 4.10) these companies will become associated companies when you marry or register your civil partnership. This may have an adverse impact on one or both companies' Corporation Tax liabilities and you might want to carry out some corporate restructuring to prevent this.

6.3   ACTION AFTER MARRIAGE OR REGISTRATION

Conversely, you may be considering some transactions which would have a tax cost if you carried them out whilst still an unmarried couple.

In these cases, it makes sense to delay the transactions until after the date of marriage or registration.

Once married or registered, rental income on jointly held property can only be shared in the proportion of actual beneficial ownership or can be deemed to be split 50/50. It can no longer be split in any other proportion.

For example, an unmarried couple may actually own the property 75/25 but share the income 60/40 by agreement, as detailed in section 4.9. Once married, the income would be deemed to be shared 50/50, with an option to elect for ACTUAL beneficial ownership – i.e. 75/25 in this case. The 60/40 option would no longer be available.

Since one possible option is removed by marriage, this may sometimes warrant some restructuring in order to achieve the desired result. Happily, such restructuring can, of course, now be carried out without any capital gains tax consequences.

The restructuring itself, however, will usually be best left until shortly after your wedding or partnership registration, as you will then be able to transfer property between yourselves free from Capital Gains Tax.

6.4   MAIN RESIDENCES

Your main residence is completely tax free while it's your main residence and for at least three years after that.

As we saw in section 4.8, as an unmarried couple you will have been able to have two main residences. This ceases on your wedding or registration day.

In many cases, you will, in fact, only have one residence between you anyway by this point, so it will make little difference.

If, however, you do still have two residences, you will now need to choose which one is to be regarded as your main residence for Capital Gains Tax purposes.

You have two years from your wedding or registration day to make this decision, which is done by making an election, in writing, addressed to 'Her Majesty's Inspector of Taxes' and sent to your tax office (with a copy to your spouse or registered civil partner's tax office). Both of you must sign the election.

There is no particular prescribed form for the election, although the following example wording would be suitable for inclusion:

> 'In accordance with section 222(5) Taxation of Chargeable Gains Act 1992, we hereby nominate [Property] as our main residence with effect from [Date*].'

* - The first such election which you make will automatically be treated as coming into effect from your wedding or registration date. It is this first election to which the two year time limit applies.

However, once an election is in place, it may subsequently be changed by a further written notice given to the Inspector under the same procedure, at any time.

It's important to point out that a new election may be given *retrospective* effect, if desired, by up to two years. This allows you to do some creative tax planning.

Example

Tina has a small flat in Southampton where she works. In September 2005, she marries Max who has a house on the Isle of Wight. Tina continues to spend weekday nights in her own flat but lives with Max in the Isle of Wight house at the weekend.

In August 2007, Tina and Max realise that the Isle of Wight house has appreciated in value significantly since Max bought it. Tina's mainland flat has not increased in value quite so significantly. They therefore elect, before the expiry of the two year time limit, that the island house is their main residence for Capital Gains Tax purposes.

In 2009 Max sells the Isle of Wight house at a substantial gain, which is completely tax free.

Note in this example that Tina's flat will not be counted as her main residence backdated to September 2005 when they got married.

However, should she now sell the flat it will still be tax free because her final three years of ownership will still be covered by the principal private residence exemption.

Tax Tip

As soon as Max and Tina decided to sell the Isle of Wight house, they should have submitted a new main residence election nominating the Southampton flat as their main residence, *with effect from a date two years previously.*

This would give an extra two years of principal private residence exemption on the flat, whilst leaving the Isle of Wight house tax free as long as they sell it within one year.

Why one year? Because main residence relief gives you those three extra 'bonus years'. By nominating the Southampton flat with effect from two years previously gives them just one more year to sell the Isle of Wight house tax free.

Regardless of any election, however, a property may only be a main residence for principal private residence purposes if it is, in fact, one or both of the couple's own private residence. Hence, a property being let out cannot be covered by the principal private residence exemption whilst it is being let. (It would nevertheless still usually be exempt for the final three years of ownership and would also attract the private letting exemption, if it were the owner's main residence at some other time.)

In the absence of any election, the question of which property is the couple's main residence has to be determined on the facts of the case. Revenue & Customs may often determine the position to the couple's detriment. Clearly then, it is <u>always</u> wise to make the election!

As a quick guide, in most cases where each member of the couple had their own main residence prior to the date of marriage or registration of their civil partnership, the best way for them to maximise their overall tax reliefs would be to do the following **after** they marry or register the civil partnership:

- Put both former main residences into joint names together.

- Both live in each property as their main residence (together) at some period, or

- If both properties continue to be private residences (i.e. not let out, etc), use main residence elections to ensure that each property has main residence status for them both at some time.

Chapter 7

Tax Planning During Marriage or Civil Partnership

7.1 A BRIEF HISTORY OF TAX AND MARRIAGE

Income Tax was introduced by Pitt the Younger in 1799 as a temporary measure to finance the escalating cost of the Napoleonic Wars. Napoleon, as many readers will know, escaped from Elba after his first defeat and had to be beaten once more, at Waterloo. That, of course, was in 1815, but Her Majesty's Treasury are playing it safe and keeping Income Tax going just in case old Bonaparte ever decides to try it on for a third time.

I jest, of course, but the serious point is that the roots of our current taxation system go back more than two centuries. Back to a time when a woman was considered to be a mere chattel and a married man was given a higher personal allowance for Income Tax purposes to reflect the cost of 'keeping' this 'burdensome chattel'. (Ladies – I do hope you can read the irony between the lines here.)

Well, all that may have made sense in 1799, but, sad to say, the same system continued largely unaltered until 5th April 1990 (a mere 15 years ago!). Throughout this period of almost 200 years, a married woman was effectively a nonentity for UK tax purposes – all her income was, in law, treated as belonging to her husband.

Because the Georgian architects of the UK tax system viewed married women as mere chattels, they therefore viewed married men as the only part of the marriage of any importance. But this is where the good part comes in. Over two centuries this approach has evolved into the current position where married couples are effectively regarded as a *single unit* for most UK tax purposes.

This approach, in turn, lies at the heart of some of the main tax advantages of marriage, including the complete exemptions from Capital Gains Tax and Inheritance Tax on all transfers of assets between most married couples.

Fortunately, the introduction of 'separate taxation' from 6th April 1990, whereby married women finally became taxpayers in their own right, did little to change the general approach to married couples as a single unit for UK tax purposes. Ten years later, the subsequent abolition of the 'Married Couples Allowance' for taxpayers born after 5th April 1935 also left this general principle unaltered.

Finally, to bring our story fully up to date, Gordon Brown confirmed in his most recent Budget Statement on 16th March 2005 that, from 5th December 2005, same sex couples in registered civil partnerships are to enjoy all of the same tax benefits (and share all of the same tax pitfalls) as married couples.

7.2   ASSET TRANSFERS BETWEEN HUSBAND AND WIFE OR REGISTERED CIVIL PARTNERS

For most Capital Gains Tax purposes, the transfer of an asset from one member of a married couple, or registered civil partnership, to the other is effectively ignored.

The most important consequence of this is that no Capital Gains Tax can ever arise on such a transfer.

The transfer is regarded as having taken place at such a price as gives rise to no gain and no loss. In a great many cases, this is effectively the same as ignoring the transfer altogether and pretending that the spouse or partner who receives the asset is the one who acquired it in the first place.

To say that the transferee stands in the transferor's shoes is a reasonable approximation of the Capital Gains Tax consequences of such a transfer but readers must be aware that the correct position is subtly different. Whilst this difference may be subtle, it would be unwise to ignore it, as it can make enormous differences in some cases.

We will look at these finer subtleties later in this chapter but, before then, let's take a look at a fairly simple example.

Example

George owns a small house in Swansea which he bought in 1999 for £50,000. He has rented it out since purchase and, by January 2006, it is worth £175,000.

On 1st February 2006, George gives the Swansea house to his wife Mildred. In March 2007, Mildred sells the house for £190,000.

The result of this is that George is treated as having sold the house to Mildred for £50,000 – the price he paid for it.

Mildred is therefore treated as having made a capital gain of £140,000 (£190,000 less £50,000) before any exemptions or reliefs. The value of the house at the date of the transfer from George to Mildred is completely irrelevant.

7.3 MARGINAL RATE TAX PLANNING

Naturally, the ability to transfer assets to your husband, wife or registered civil partner free from Capital Gains Tax provides huge potential for tax planning.

Throughout Chapters 2 and 3, we saw many examples of cases where transferring the underlying assets would enable the income or capital gains which those assets generate to effectively be moved to a lower marginal rate of tax.

The fact that the transfer itself does not result in Capital Gains Tax makes all of this marginal rate tax planning far easier to achieve.

7.4   MAIN RESIDENCE EXEMPTIONS

One area where great savings may be made through transfers to your spouse or registered civil partner is in the area of Principal Private Residence Relief and its companion relief, Private Letting Relief.

Principal private residence relief is available on any property which is regarded as your main residence (i.e. your home) or has been your main residence at any time during your ownership.

As I have mentioned before, your former main residence will also be exempt for the last three years of your ownership.

Additionally, if a property that has been your main residence is let out as private residential accommodation it will also qualify for Private Letting Relief.

Private Letting Relief is given as the *lowest* of:

i)   The amount of gain already exempted under principal private residence relief,
ii)   The gain arising as a consequence of the letting period, and
iii)   £40,000.

Usually, it is the lower of (i) and (iii), especially if the property has been let out ever since you ceased to reside in it.

The key thing about the statutory £40,000 limit, however, is that it is given on a *per person* basis. This gives a couple the opportunity to double the value of this relief.

So far, all of this would apply equally to an unmarried couple who had owned the property jointly since purchase and had both lived in it together as their main residence at some stage.

However, a spouse or registered civil partner will often be eligible for ALL the same reliefs as their partner when calculating the Capital Gains Tax on the sale of that partner's former home – even if they've only recently obtained ownership.

This, in effect, gives the couple backdated relief, as one partner may not have owned the property for very long.

Let's look at this in practice.

Example

George buys a house on 1st April 1998 for £200,000 and occupies it as his own main residence. In June 1999, he marries Gracie and she moves in with him.

On 1st April 2000, the couple move out of the house and George begins to rent it out.

On 1st April 2006, George sells the house for £500,000. He is a higher rate taxpayer.

The house is covered by the principal private residence exemption for the two years that it was George's main residence plus the last three years of his ownership, giving him a total of five years exemption out of his total ownership period of eight years. In other words, five eighths of his gain will be tax free thanks to this relief.

He is also eligible for taper relief at 30% as he has owned the house for eight years.

His Capital Gains Tax calculation will therefore be as follows:

Sale proceeds		*£500,000*
Less: Purchase cost		*£200,000*
		£300,000
Principal Private Residence Relief for 5 years out of 8		*£187,500*
		£112,500
Private letting relief:		*£40,000*
		£72,500
Taper Relief @	*30%*	*£21,750*
		£50,750
Annual exemption		*£8,500*
Taxable gain		*£42,250*

George's Capital Gains Tax bill, at 40%, will therefore be £16,900.

However, if George put the house into joint names with Gracie before selling it, the Capital Gains Tax calculation for each of them would be as follows:

Sale proceeds (half)		*£250,000*
Less: Purchase cost (half)		*£100,000*
		£150,000
Principal Private Residence Relief for 5 years out of 8		*£93,750*
		£56,250
Private letting relief:		*£40,000*
		£16,250
Taper Relief @	*30%*	*£4,875*
		£11,375
Annual exemption		*£8,500*
Taxable gain		*£2,875*

George's own Capital Gains Tax liability will now be only £1,150. Gracie's will be between £366 and £1,150, depending on the level of her income for the year.

In any case, the transfer of the house to Gracie will save the couple at least £14,600.

When transferring a property to your spouse or registered civil partner for these purposes it is vital to bear in mind my earlier comments regarding settlements (section 2.9) and beneficial ownership (section 2.16).

If you put the property into joint ownership as tenants in common, or into pro indivisio ownership if it is located in Scotland, you will not have to put it into equal joint shares and could choose **any other split** which may be more advantageous.

Another very important point here is that, for this planning to work, the transferee spouse or civil partner must have occupied the property as **their** main residence at some time during the transferor's ownership.

It does not matter that they did not own a share of the property when it was their main residence, or even if the couple were unmarried at that time, but it **must** have been their main residence.

Example Revisited

If George had not met Gracie until 2001 and she had therefore never occupied the property which had been his home prior to April 2000, her Capital Gains Tax liability on a sale of a joint half share in the property in April 2006 would then be as follows:

Sale proceeds (half)		£250,000
Less: Purchase cost (half)		£100,000
		£150,000
Taper Relief @	30%	£45,000
		£105,000
Annual exemption		£8,500
Taxable gain		£96,500

Clearly this would be quite disastrous and could cost the couple up to an extra £22,850 in Capital Gains Tax.

Tax Tip

If your spouse or registered civil partner has never lived in the property concerned, a major tax saving can still be achieved if you both move back into the property for a reasonable period prior to sale.

As for what a reasonable period is, see the Taxcafe.co.uk guide *'How To Avoid Property Tax'.*

It is also worth noting that in this scenario, the transferee spouse or civil partner will be entitled to the same rate of taper relief as the transferor. This is not always the case for every type of transferred asset, however, as we shall see in the next section.

7.5 HAVE YOUR CAKE AND EAT IT

Income Tax savings can also be generated by transferring an investment property into either *joint* names with your spouse or registered civil partner, or into the *sole* name of the spouse or registered civil partner with a lower overall income.

As we saw in section 2.14, in the right circumstances, moving rental income from one spouse or registered civil partner to another in this way can save over £8,000 in Income Tax *each year*.

However, in order to comply with the settlements legislation, this form of tax planning is not effective unless beneficial title in the property is genuinely transferred. But not everyone trusts their spouse or registered civil partner enough to simply hand over the title to their property (or half of it)!

For Income Tax purposes, at least, there is a way to solve this dilemma. Where property is held jointly by a married couple or civil partners, there is an automatic presumption for Income Tax purposes, that the income arises in equal shares.

This 50/50 split will continue to be applied unless and until the couple jointly elect for the income to be split in accordance with the true beneficial title in the property.

Hence, where a property owner who is married or in a registered civil partnership wants to save Income Tax on their rental profits without giving up too much of their title to the property, what they should do is:

- Put the property into joint names with their spouse or registered civil partner. If the property is in England or Wales, a Tenancy in Common should be used.

- Retain 99% of the beneficial ownership themselves and transfer only 1% to their spouse or registered civil partner.

  AND

- Simply never elect for the income to be split in accordance with the true beneficial title.

Conversely

Conversely, of course, there will be cases where the actual beneficial ownership split is preferable for tax purposes.

In these cases, the election to split the income on an actual basis should usually be made.

Beware though that, once made, this election is irreversible.

7.6   TAPER RELIEF PLANNING

As we saw in section 2.22, taper relief is dependent on both the length of ownership of the asset and whether the asset qualifies as a business asset.

For transfers between spouses or registered civil partners, the transferee will be treated as having held the asset for the combined period of holding of both partners.

Example

Jill buys some quoted shares in January 1999 and gives them to her husband Jack in December 2005. Neither Jill nor Jack work for the company which issued the shares and so they qualify for non-business asset taper relief.

Jack sells the shares in February 2007.

Jack will be eligible for taper relief on the gain on these shares at the rate of 30% as he is treated as if he had held them for eight years.

So, the length of ownership transfers to the transferee spouse or registered civil partner.

However, the *nature* of the asset for taper relief purposes, (i.e. whether or not it is regarded as a business asset) does not transfer.

Shares and Securities

In the case of shares and securities, how much taper relief they qualify for depends on the spouse or civil partner making the ultimate disposal.

Example

Rita owns some shares in Hayworth plc which she bought on the stock market three years ago. She herself has no other connection with Hayworth plc.

If she sells these shares, she will only be eligible for taper relief at 5%. Even if she hangs on to them for another seven years, her taper relief will still only amount to 40%.

Instead of selling the shares, however, Rita transfers them to her husband Errol. Errol is an employee of Hayworth plc and is therefore entitled to business asset taper relief on the shares.

He is also already entitled to the 75% maximum rate of relief as he is treated as having held the shares since Rita bought them, which is over two years ago.

We can readily see how such a transfer could save a married couple or registered civil partnership large amounts of Capital Gains Tax.

Other Assets

The rules for transfers of other types of asset are slightly different.

Generally, other types of asset are only treated as business assets for any period during the couple's combined period of ownership when the relevant asset qualified as a business asset in the hands of the partner who actually held it at the time.

There is an exception to this rule when the asset is transferred to a spouse or registered civil partner and, prior to that transfer, it had already been used in a trade carried on by the transferee. In such a case, the transferee is able to treat the transferred asset as a business asset for the period during which it was being used in their own trade.

Changes made to the taper relief rules with effect from 6th April 2004 mean that this exception will only be of benefit in the case of assets already held by one of the couple prior to that date. For periods of ownership after that date, an asset would in any case qualify as a business asset if it were being used in a trade carried on by the spouse or registered civil partner of the owner (or, indeed, any other individual, as well as various other business entities, as detailed in Appendix E).

Example

Mark bought some small retail premises on 6th April 1998 and has rented them to his partner Bridget ever since. Bridget has been running a sweet shop from the premises owned by Mark throughout this period.

Bridget and Mark got married in 2004 and, in late 2005, she gives Mark the happy news that she is expecting.

The couple decide that Bridget should give up work to look after the baby and therefore plan to sell the shop early in the 2006/2007 tax year.

If Mark sells the property himself, he will only be entitled to the more generous business asset taper relief on the proportion of his period of ownership falling after 6th April 2004. (This is the date when the business asset definition was widened.)

If, for example, this sale took place on 6th April 2006 then Mark would be able to claim business asset taper relief at 75% on just two eighths of his capital gain. He would be able to claim 30% non-business asset taper relief on the other six eighths of his gain.

If Mark transfers the shop to Bridget, however, then when she sells it, she will be entitled to the full 75% taper relief because the shop has always been used in her business. (As long as she continues to use it in her business up to the date of sale. Even if it is vacant for a short period of a few weeks before the sale, only a small part of the taper relief would be lost.)

On a gain of, say, £100,000, this would save the couple up to £13,500 in Capital Gains Tax.

Tax Tip

It will almost always be worth transferring an asset to a spouse or registered civil partner when they are using it in their own trading business.

In addition to the possibility of improving the taper relief situation, the spouse or civil partner using the asset in their trading business would be eligible for Capital Gains Tax hold over relief and also rollover relief on replacement of business assets on a sale of the asset.

The asset would also generally be exempt from Inheritance Tax if held by the partner using it in their own trade.

Chapter 8

Separation and Divorce

8.1 THE END OF THE LINE

As we saw in Chapters 5 and 6, getting married or entering into a registered civil partnership causes some very important changes in your tax status.

It naturally follows that separation and divorce will cause some equally important changes.

Hence, many of the comments in this guide aimed at those contemplating marriage or a registered civil partnership, will have similar application for those contemplating divorce or separation. It is, however, perhaps rather less common for anyone to divorce or separate for tax reasons.

8.2 WHEN DOES SEPARATION OCCUR?

It is generally accepted that a person ceases to be your spouse if you are legally separated from them, or separated from them in circumstances which are likely to become permanent.

Hence, if your husband walks out one day leaving a note saying "I need some time to think things over, I'll be back in a couple of weeks", then you are probably still married as far as UK tax law is concerned (at least for the time being, anyway).

If, on the other hand, you get a postcard from Canada saying that he never wants to see you again, you are probably no longer married for tax purposes.

As ever, real life so rarely gives us such clear-cut examples and each individual case has to be looked at on its own merits.

The few cases regarding this issue which have reached the courts show us that it is the couple's intentions which will decide the matter.

In one case back in 1948, it was claimed that a couple should no longer be regarded as married because the husband had been abroad on war work for three years. The case was dismissed – establishing the principle that a couple who are merely physically separated from each other remain married for tax purposes unless they intend to make that separation permanent.

On the other hand, in a more recent case, a couple who had decided to divorce but who, due to financial constraints, continued to live as two separate households under the same roof, were regarded as no longer married from the moment that they decided to separate, even though there was little physical separation between them.

In future, it is likely that the same principles regarding separation will be applied to registered civil partnerships so that the partnership's tax status will cease in the event of a legal separation or separation under circumstances which are likely to become permanent.

8.3   WHAT HAPPENS AFTER SEPARATION?

Most tax reliefs tend to continue to apply *until the end of the tax year* in which separation takes place.

This is very useful since the exact date of separation is not always absolutely clear and the law therefore allows us merely to decide on a 'year of separation' for most tax purposes.

Furthermore, despite the above comments, some tax reliefs do continue to apply up until the end of the tax year in which a decree nisi is granted.

Wealth Warning

Separated couples need to be very careful, as they remain 'connected persons' (see section 5.8) for tax purposes right up until the day of their decree absolute. What this means in practice is that most of the disadvantages of marriage tend to linger on long after the advantages have ceased!

8.4   ASSET TRANSFERS IN THE YEAR OF SEPARATION

The Capital Gains Tax exemption for transfers between spouses or registered civil partners will normally remain in force for the whole of the tax year of separation.

If, however, a decree absolute is granted within that same tax year, the Capital Gains Tax exemption ends on the date that the decree is granted.

Whilst you may not **want** to transfer any assets to your spouse or registered civil partner under these circumstances, the continuation of the exemption gives you the opportunity to pass over wealth without any Capital Gains Tax liability for a short period after you separate.

This will be very useful when assets need to be transferred as part of a separation agreement.

I realise that tax considerations will rarely dictate what goes on in people's personal lives but, from a tax planning perspective, it does make financial sense to try to delay separation until early into a new tax year. This will then give you almost twelve months to do some vital Capital Gains Tax planning.

8.5   THE MARITAL HOME

The good news is that, after separating, you will again be able to have your own individual main residence for principal private residence relief purposes.

Alternatively, however, if you have not claimed any principal private residence relief on a main residence elsewhere in the interim, your former marital home will continue to be exempt as long as your ex-spouse or ex-registered civil partner continues to use it as their main residence.

Chapter 9

Older Couples

9.1   THE 'MARRIED COUPLES ALLOWANCE'

Between 1990 and the year 2000, every married couple was entitled to the Married Couples Allowance. It wasn't worth much; it was a mere £1,970 in its final year and provided a tax credit at just 10%. Hence, the maximum saving was a paltry £197. Still, it was better than a 'poke in the eye with a sharp stick'.

But then on 6th April 2000 it was taken away from everyone born after 5th April 1935.

Today, the allowance provides a maximum saving of up to £597.50 for older married couples (where one of the couple is aged 75 or more).

In his Budget speech on 16th March 2005, Gordon Brown specifically confirmed that this allowance would extend to same sex couples in registered civil partnerships from 5th December 2005. Clearly, a name change will soon be in order for the allowance.

One name they won't be using is the old nickname of 'Male Chauvinist Allowance' which was coined some years ago in response to the fact that the allowance actually had to be claimed by the husband. Now that at least one of the couple must be at least 70 years old, the furore over the sexist nature of this allowance has died down somewhat. (The Government's idea seems to be that women aged 70 or more are, by now, well and truly used to a male-biased world!)

It nevertheless does remain one of the last pieces of sexist tax legislation which we have in the UK, as the Married Couples Allowance must still be claimed by the husband where it is available.

As for registered same sex civil partnerships, it has yet to be determined which member of the partnership will claim any 'Married Couples Allowance' which may be due.

The maximum possible benefit which any member of a civil partnership will be able to derive from the 'Married Couples Allowance' for the 2005/2006 tax year will be just £249. Even this will require the couple to have registered their partnership on the first possible day, 5th December 2005, as well as one of them being at least 75 years old by 5th April 2006 and having total annual income of no more than £19,500. (Sounds a bit like the conditions for getting credit in my local pub – 'the customer must be aged 85 or over and both parents must attend in person to verify this fact'.)

My suspicion, at present, is that the Government may change the rules so that the highest earner in the couple must claim the allowance. We will see the disadvantage of this in the next section. In order to be fair to everyone, they will undoubtedly apply this new rule to both civil partnerships and married couples. In other words, as usual, when cornered their response to any perceived unfairness in the tax system is not to give the same advantage to everyone, but rather to take the advantage away altogether!

9.2   CALCULATING THE ALLOWANCE

For married couples, or same sex partners in a registered civil partnership, where one or both of them were born before 6th April 1935, the 'Married Couples Allowance' is given in the form of a 10% tax credit on the following amounts of income:

- Where the older member of the couple was born before 6th April 1935, but is aged under 75: £5,905
- Where the older member of the couple is aged 75 or more: £5,975.

Unlike most allowances in the tax system, the Married Couples Allowance often gets an annual increase in excess of the rate of retail price inflation.

Where applicable, the Married Couples Allowance is given *in addition* to your personal allowance.

Only one 'Married Couples Allowance' is available per couple.

It remains available, for the whole of the tax year of divorce, separation or death of a spouse or registered civil partner. A suitably reduced proportion may be claimed in the year of marriage or registration of the civil partnership.

Tax Tip – 'Grab a Granny'

Note that the Married Couples Allowance is available whenever the older member of the couple was born before 6th April 1935.

Hence, whatever age **you** are, you can qualify for Married Couples Allowance by marrying, or entering into a registered civil partnership with, someone who is old enough.

With a maximum tax saving available of just £597.50 per annum, however, it is rather questionable whether it is worth marrying or entering a registered civil partnership for this reason alone!

Each of the age limits described above is applied according to the taxpayer's age at the *end of the tax year.* Hence a married man whose wife was born on 3rd April 1931 will be entitled to the higher Married Couples Allowance of £5,975 for the 2005/2006 tax year.

The Married Couples allowance is progressively withdrawn when the taxpayer's income exceeds £19,500 per annum.

Withdrawal is at the rate of £1 for every £2 of income over this threshold. This creates a higher effective marginal tax rate for taxpayers with income between £19,500 and somewhere between £23,890 and £31,540, depending on age and marital status.

Those eligible for the 'Married Couples Allowance' throughout the whole year will always still be entitled to a minimum allowance of at least £2,280 for 2005/2006.

It's also important to point out that *all* taxpayers aged 65 or more at the end of the tax year also get a higher, 'age-related' personal allowance. This will be withdrawn first, before the Married Couples Allowance.

Example 1

Ashton is aged 63 and is married to Demi, who was born on 1ˢᵗ April 1935. Ashton is therefore entitled to the Married Couples Allowance for 2005/2006.

If Ashton's total income for 2005/2006 is not in excess of £19,500, he will get the full allowance of £5,905.

For every additional £2 of income Ashton receives over £19,500, however, he will lose £1 of his Married Couples Allowance.

Once Ashton has income of £26,750, his Married Couples Allowance will have been reduced to the minimum level of £2,280, giving a tax saving of just £228.

As explained in the previous section, the Married Couples Allowance must currently be claimed by the husband. Hence, it is the husband's income which must be considered when calculating whether the 'Married Couples Allowance' should be withdrawn.

The minimum amount of the Married Couples Allowance (£2,280 for 2005/2006) can be transferred to the wife (by joint election) or can be shared between the couple equally (on a claim by the wife).

Additionally, any further part of the Married Couples Allowance which cannot be used because the husband's income is not high enough, may also be claimed by the wife if she has sufficient capacity to utilise it.

Tax Tip

As explained above, the Married Couples Allowance is withdrawn by reference to the husband's income.

Hence, where possible, it will often be better to ensure that the wife gets a greater income than her husband, thus avoiding the loss of the available Married Couples Allowance.

How these same rules will be applied to registered civil partnerships is yet to be seen.

9.3   YEAR OF MARRIAGE OR REGISTRATION

As mentioned in section 9.2, a partial allowance is given in the year of marriage or in which a civil partnership is registered.

This partial allowance is based on the number of months in the tax year for which the taxpayer is married or in a registered civil partnership.

9.4 WIDOWS, WIDOWERS AND SURVIVING CIVIL PARTNERS

A full allowance is given for the tax year in which one person (or even both, for that matter) dies. There is no restriction if the survivor re-marries or enters a new registered civil partnership during the year.

There used to be an extra allowance available to any surviving spouse in the year *after* their partner's death. Sadly, this is no longer available.

9.5 POLYGAMOUS MARRIAGES

Those whose faith permits them to have more than one spouse are still restricted to just one Married Couples Allowance in each tax year.

The leading case on the subject dates back to the 1970's and involves the case of Mr Nabi, a Moslem, who eventually won his claim for higher personal allowances after separating from his first wife in the UK on the grounds that he also had a second wife whom he had married in Pakistan.

The polygamous marriage was only recognised in this case because the taxpayer was domiciled in a country where polygamous marriages were legal. Had Mr Nabi been UK domiciled, the outcome may have been different, so this rule is perhaps not something which everyone should rely on.

9.6 WHY ARE OLDER COUPLES DIFFERENT?

Depending on age and marital status, older taxpayers have a variety of different marginal tax rates all of which differ from those given in Chapter 2 for their younger counterparts.

The differences occur for several reasons:

i)   Taxpayers over state retirement age are not required to pay National Insurance Contributions.
ii)   Taxpayers aged 65 or more at the end of the tax year are entitled to a higher, 'age-related' personal allowance.
iii)   Those aged 75 or more at the end of the tax year get a slightly higher personal allowance than those aged 65 to 74.
iv)   Married couples, or same sex partners in a registered civil partnership, where one or both of them were born before 6th April 1935, are also entitled to the 'Married Couples Allowance'.
v)   Where one member of a married couple or registered civil partnership is aged 75 or more at the end of the tax year the 'Married Couples Allowance' is also slightly increased (see section 9.2).

To compound matters, the additional allowances under (ii) to (iv) above are reduced when the taxpayer's income exceeds an 'income limit' (£19,500 for 2005/2006).

State retirement age is, of course, also different for men (65) and women (60).

Class 1 National Insurance Contributions on employment income only cease for salary payments made after the employee passes state retirement age. Employer's secondary contributions continue to be payable regardless of the employee's age.

Older self-employed taxpayers have to pay Class 2 National Insurance Contributions right up until the week before they reach state retirement age and still have to pay Class 4 National Insurance Contributions in full for any tax year during any part of which they were still below state retirement age. (Those with a 6th April birthday get to stop paying National Insurance a whole year before those born a day later.)

9.7 MARGINAL TAX RATES FOR OLDER COUPLES

In Chapter 2, we explored the importance of understanding each member of the couple's marginal tax rates when undertaking any tax planning based around sharing the couple's mutual wealth.

This principle remains unaltered for older couples despite the complications caused by the factors described in the previous section.

These various factors, however, cause an absolute plethora of possible marginal rates and it would therefore be impossible to reproduce all of them here.

Nevertheless, set out below are some of the most common marginal tax rates applying to older taxpayers.

All of the tables set out below operate in the same way as described previously in Chapter 2 (i.e. under the 'layer system').

Women Aged between 60 and 64

The marginal rates of tax for 2005/2006 for women aged between 60 and 64 at the end of the tax year are as follows:

		Employment	Self-Employment	Employer's National Insurance Contributions
First	£4,895	0%	0%	0%
£4,895 -	£6,985	10%	10%	12.8%
£6,985 -	£37,295	22%	22%	12.8%
Over	£37,295	40%	40%	12.8%

Notes
- This table assumes that the taxpayer is not entitled to claim Married Couples Allowance for the year.

- National Insurance will continue to be due on any employment income received in the part of the year prior to the taxpayer's 60th birthday.
- For women aged under 60 on 6th April 2005, revert to the table in section 2.5 for self-employment income.
- For other types of income, the position is unaltered from that shown in Chapter 2.

Unmarried Persons Aged between 65 and 74, & Married Persons Aged 65 to 69

The marginal rates of tax for 2005/2006 for:

a) unmarried taxpayers aged between 65 and 74 at the end of the tax year, and

b) married taxpayers and taxpayers in registered civil partnerships aged 65 or more at the end of the tax year but where neither member of the couple was born before 6th April 1935,

are as follows:

			Employment, Self-Employment & Rental Income	Interest & Other Investment Income	Foreign Dividends
First		£7,090	0%	0%	0%
£7,090	-	£9,180	10%	10%	10%
£9,180	-	£19,500	22%	20%	10%
£19,500	-	£23,890	33%	30%	15%
£23,890	-	£37,295	22%	20%	10%
Over		£37,295	40%	40%	32.5%

Notes

- National Insurance will continue to be due on any employment income received by men in the part of the year prior to their 65th birthday.
- Employer's secondary National Insurance Contributions continue to be payable at normal rates.

- National Insurance will also continue to be payable on self-employment income received by men aged under 65 on 6th April 2005.

Married Persons Aged 70 or more or Aged 65 to 69 and with a Spouse or Civil Partner aged 70 or more

The marginal rates of tax for 2005/2006 for married taxpayers and taxpayers in registered civil partnerships where:
  a) both members of the couple are aged between 65 and 74 at the end of the tax year, and
  b) one or both of the couple was born before 6th April 1935,
and where the taxpayer themselves is the one eligible to claim the Married Couples Allowance (normally the husband in the case of a married couple, but see section 9.2 above), are as follows:

		Employment, Self-Employment & Rental Income	Interest & Other Investment Income	Foreign Dividends
First		£9,180	0%	0%	0%
£9,180	-	£12,995	12%	10%	0%
£12,995	-	£19,500	22%	20%	10%
£19,500	-	£23,890	33%	30%	15%
£23,890	-	£31,140	27%	25%	15%
£31,140	-	£37,295	22%	20%	10%
Over		£37,295	40%	40%	32.5%

Notes
- National Insurance will continue to be due on any employment income received by men in the part of the year prior to their 65th birthday.
- Employer's secondary National Insurance Contributions continue to be payable at normal rates.

180

- National Insurance will also continue to be payable on self-employment income received by men aged under 65 on 6th April 2005.

Wealth Warning

As before, in Chapter 2, these tables are only a rough guide and, to carry out marginal rate planning effectively, it is essential to look at the impact on each member of the couple's overall tax position.

With the withdrawal of age-related allowances when income exceeds £19,500, this is probably even more important than ever for older taxpayers.

UK Dividends

When a basic rate taxpayer aged 65 or more at the end of the tax year receives UK dividends, the dividends themselves continue to be tax free.

However, when the taxpayer's total income exceeds the income limit (£19,500 for 2005/2006), the consequent reduction of the taxpayer's higher, age-related personal allowance can cause an effective marginal rate of tax on the dividends received of up to 12.2%, depending on which other types of income the taxpayer has.

Once the age-related element of the personal allowance has been used, anyone entitled to the married couples allowance will also generally continue to suffer an effective tax rate of 5.6% on their UK dividend income, until that allowance too has been reduced to its minimum level.

Capital Gains

The marginal rates of tax applying to capital gains, as already set out in section 2.16, are unaltered by a taxpayer's age.

Chapter 10

Inheritance Tax

10.1 INHERITANCE TAX & COUPLES

Inheritance Tax is, of course, an enormously complex subject in its own right which is covered in some depth in the Taxcafe.co.uk guide *'How To Avoid Inheritance Tax'*.

An examination of tax planning for couples would not, however, be complete without at least a brief summary of the implications of Inheritance Tax for couples.

10.2 INHERITANCE TAX & MARRIAGE OR CIVIL PARTNERSHIPS

The key point is this:

All transfers of property to your spouse or registered civil partner are completely exempt from Inheritance Tax.

This covers both lifetime transfers and transfers made on death. Any property left to your spouse or registered civil partner on your death is therefore usually completely free of Inheritance Tax.

Exception – Spouses/Civil Partners with Separate Domicile

Where one of you is UK Domiciled and the other is not, the general exemption for transfers between spouses or registered civil partners is restricted.

In this case, only the first £55,000 of transfers from the UK Domiciled spouse or civil partner to the foreign Domiciled spouse or registered civil partner is exempt.

There is no restriction on transfers in the opposite direction – why would there be? - such transfers would potentially increase Revenue & Customs' tax haul.

The concept of Domicile is explained further in section 11.3.

However, any person who has been UK resident for at least 17 out of the last 20 years will usually be treated as UK Domiciled for Inheritance Tax purposes, even if they remain non-domiciled for other purposes.

Other Exceptions

The general exemption for transfers between spouses or registered civil partners is also restricted in a few other circumstances. For example, the exemption may be lost where:

- The transfer only takes effect after the expiry of someone else's interest in the asset or some other period of time.

Tax Tip

It is, however, acceptable to have a condition in your Will that your spouse or registered civil partner must survive you by a certain period before becoming entitled to the asset.

- The transfer is dependent on a condition which is not satisfied within twelve months.

10.3   USING YOUR NIL RATE BAND

As explained in the previous section, property left to your spouse or registered civil partner is usually exempt from Inheritance Tax. However, utilising this exemption to the full is *not* always a good idea.

Hence, the first question I ask anyone who comes to me for Inheritance Tax planning advice is "are you married?" (In future, my second question may well be "are you in a registered civil partnership?")

This is because every married couple or registered civil partnership can save up to £110,000 in Inheritance Tax for their family by following a fairly straightforward planning strategy.

All that this strategy involves is ensuring that the first one of the couple to die uses their Nil Rate Band on transfers to someone **other** than their spouse or civil partner.

The Nil Rate Band is currently £275,000, so utilising it to save Inheritance Tax at 40% will leave your family £110,000 better off.

Without this strategy, the couple is simply wasting one of their Nil Rate Bands and thus volunteering to give the Government an extra £110,000!

Example

Eddie dies in December 2005, leaving his net estate worth £2,000,000 to his daughter Carrie. After setting off Eddie's Nil Rate Band, Carrie will have an Inheritance Tax bill of £690,000. (£2,000,000 - £275,000 = £1,725,000 x 40% = £690,000)

Eddie was, in fact, a widower, and within his estate there was a property worth £275,000, which he had inherited from his wife Debbie, who had died in June 2005.

Since Debbie left the property to her husband and it was therefore exempt anyway, her Nil Rate Band was never used.

What Debbie should have done, instead, was to leave her property to their daughter, Carrie. No Inheritance Tax would have been payable on her death, as her property was covered by the Nil Rate Band.

But when Eddie died later in the year, his estate would have been worth £275,000 less, thus saving £110,000 of Inheritance Tax.

The non-spousal legacy (i.e. the one to Carrie in the above example) does not need to be one specific property.

It could be a whole group of assets, or simply worded as a legacy equal to the Nil Rate Band to be paid out of the general assets of the estate.

Tax Tip

When including a legacy to someone other than your spouse in your will with the intention of utilising your Nil Rate Band, it is best not to word it as a legacy for £275,000 – the *current* Nil Rate Band.

What you should do instead is draft your will so that it includes a legacy equal to whatever the Nil Rate Band happens to be at the time of your death.

That way, the amount of the legacy will automatically adjust in line with the Nil Rate Band each year. The non-spousal legacy strategy is pretty simple to follow when, like Eddie and Debbie, there are plenty of assets around.

But What if You're Not that Well Off?

The problem for most married couples or registered civil partnerships is that they can't afford to simply give their children, or other beneficiaries, £275,000 when one of them dies.

The widow, widower or surviving registered civil partner will need to retain sufficient assets to support them for the rest of their life including, in most cases, the family home.

Fortunately, there are some planning strategies available to deal with this dilemma facing the moderately wealthy couple.

The Nil Rate Band Discretionary Will Trust

A method which was very popular a few years ago was for each spouse to set up a Discretionary Trust through their will (see section 4.6 for a further explanation of Discretionary Trusts).

Assets at least equal to the Nil Rate Band would be left to the Trust. The surviving spouse would be one of the beneficiaries of the Trust and, in practice, would actually retain all the benefits of ownership of the assets in the Trust.

This was achieved by ensuring that the Trustees exercised their 'discretion' in such a way as to ensure that the surviving spouse received all of the income from the assets.

These schemes were even sometimes used to pass the deceased's share of the family home into the Discretionary Trust. However, Revenue & Customs have recently attacked these types of Discretionary Trusts on the basis that they are really 'Interest In Possession' Trusts. This means that the assets of the Trust would remain in the surviving spouse's estate for Inheritance Tax purposes, rendering this planning useless.

186

Nevertheless, the method could probably still be used where the Trust was genuinely discretionary in nature. This would necessitate avoiding the usual 'Letter of Instruction' to the Trustees stating that the surviving spouse or civil partner is to receive all income from the Trust. It would also be wise to ensure that other beneficiaries did, indeed, receive some Trust income.

The Widow's Loan Scheme

A better method is to leave all (or most) of the assets of the estate to the surviving spouse or registered civil partner as specific bequests, but leave a sum equal to the Nil Rate Band to a Discretionary Will Trust.

The surviving spouse or registered civil partner would be a beneficiary of the Trust, together with other family members.

The surviving spouse or civil partner ends up owing a sum equal to the Nil Rate Band to the Trust. What they then do is to simply execute a loan agreement for this amount in favour of the Trust.

When the surviving spouse or registered civil partner themselves dies, the amount of the loan is deductible from their estate, thus doubling the Nil Rate Band!

This scheme has the added strength that the Capital Taxes Office of the Inland Revenue has confirmed that they accept its validity, in principle, for Inheritance Tax purposes, as long as it is done properly.

'Doing it properly' includes drafting the will very carefully, ensuring that the Trustees have the power to enter into a loan agreement (instead of demanding immediate payment) and, above all, getting professional advice!

Wealth Warning

This method may not work if the funds used to acquire any of the assets left to the surviving spouse or registered civil partner had originally been given by the survivor to their now deceased spouse or partner.

10.4 INHERITANCE TAX & UNMARRIED COUPLES

If you are not married or in a registered civil partnership, there is no Inheritance Tax exemption for transfers of assets to your partner.

There is, however, no *immediate* Inheritance Tax charge on any transfers of assets or gifts which you make directly to your partner, or into a life interest trust for their benefit, during your lifetime.

Lifetime transfers into a discretionary trust may create an immediate Inheritance Tax charge though, as discussed in section 4.6.

On your death, however, broadly speaking, Inheritance Tax will be payable on the entire value of your taxable estate in excess of the Nil Rate Band PLUS the value of any lifetime gifts made in the last seven years of your life.

You would, however, be exempt from Inheritance Tax on the first £3,000 of lifetime gifts made in each tax year. Where your gifts in the year exceed this sum, you may also claim to use any previously unused element of the immediately preceding tax year's annual exemption, thus potentially exempting the first £6,000 of the year's gifts.

Tax Tip

If you want your partner to benefit from your annual Inheritance Tax exemptions, make sure that your first gifts in each new tax year are to them.

188

Also included in the Inheritance Tax calculation on your death would be any amounts which you elected to include in your estate in order to avoid any pre-owned asset charge (see section 4.11).

After deducting the Nil Rate Band, the net sum remaining will be liable to Inheritance Tax at 40%.

All in all, this could add up to a pretty nasty shock for your partner.

Example

Dean dies in June 2006, leaving his entire estate to his partner Jerry. The estate is valued at £1,000,000.

In March 2004, Dean had transferred a house worth £500,000 to Jerry.

Dean had also given Jerry £250,000 in cash in July 1999.

Jerry will suffer Inheritance Tax as follows:

Dean's Estate:	*£1,000,000*
Lifetime transfers within the last 7 years:	*£750,000*

	£1,750,000
Annual exemptions:	
1999/2000 & 1998/1999 exemptions used	
against gift of cash July 1999	*6,000*
2003/2004 & 2002/2003 exemptions used	
against gift of house March 2004	*6,000*

	£1,738,000
Nil Rate Band (increased with inflation)	*£285,000*

	£1,453,000
	=========
Inheritance Tax @ 40%	*£581,200*

There are many ways to reduce the Inheritance Tax burden on your partner, including:

- Maximising the proportion of your assets which qualify for business property relief (broadly similar to assets which qualify as business assets for Capital Gains Tax hold over relief purposes – see section 4.4),
- Using your annual Inheritance Tax exemptions for lifetime transfers,
- Making regular gifts out of income, and
- Setting up discretionary trusts every seven years.

By far the simplest way to protect your partner from Inheritance Tax on your death, however, is to marry them or enter a registered civil partnership with them.

Deathbed marriages (and, in future, civil partnership registrations) can save Millions in Inheritance Tax but, you should ask yourself, is it really wise to leave it to the last minute?

10.5   INHERITANCE TAX PLANNING ON MARRIAGE OR REGISTRATION

When you 'name the day', you might want to mention to your family that this is a good opportunity for them to do some Inheritance Tax planning of their own, since gifts in consideration of marriage, or registration of a civil partnership, are exempt from Inheritance Tax up to the following limits:

- Parents: £5,000
- Grandparents, Great-Grandparents, etc: £2,500
- One party to the other: £2,500
- Other Donors: £1,000

All of the above limits apply on an individual basis and the relationships referred to must be to one of the parties to the marriage or civil partnership.

Hence, for example, the groom could receive £5,000 from **each** of his parents, plus £2,500 from **each** of his grandparents and £1,000 from **all** of his aunts and uncles and the bride could receive the same from her family.

Alternatively, the bride's family could make their gifts to the groom or the groom's family could make their gifts to the bride.

The same goes for the families of civil partners when they legally register their partnership.

Additionally, within this same exemption (and within the same overriding limits as set out above), gifts could be made into a trust for the benefit of:

- The bride, groom or civil partners
- Children of the marriage or partnership
- Future spouses or registered civil partners of the children of the marriage or partnership being registered
- A future spouse or registered civil partner of either party to the marriage or partnership being registered
- Children of any subsequent marriage or registered civil partnership of either party to this marriage or partnership being registered and future spouses or registered civil partners of those children

I think that covers everyone.

Gifts in consideration of marriage or registration of a civil partnership must be made on, or shortly before, the marriage or registration, in order to fall within the exemption.

The gifts must be fully effective when the marriage or registration takes place. For example, "I give you my property at Blackacre on condition that you marry my daughter."

Where the gifts exceed the limits shown above, the excess may be covered by the annual exemption, if available.

Chapter 11

Non-Resident & Non-Domiciled Partners

11.1 OPPORTUNITY KNOCKS

Where one partner is non-UK Resident or non-UK Domiciled, this provides a large number of additional tax planning opportunities not available to other couples.

Ideally then, the couple should try to arrange their financial affairs in order to maximise the benefit of one partner's special tax status.

Subject to the usual question of whether you trust your partner, of course.

Where a partner's special tax status is being exploited, Revenue & Customs can be expected to be extra vigilant when it comes to issues such as the settlements legislation and beneficial ownership.

Furthermore, additional anti-avoidance legislation provides that the income (but not capital gains) from assets transferred to a non-UK Resident or non-UK Domiciled partner may, under certain circumstances, continue to be taxed in the hands of the person making the transfer.

11.2 NON-RESIDENT PARTNERS

A non-UK resident partner does not pay UK Capital Gains Tax.

Any capital gains which you can get into their hands should therefore be completely tax free.

Married persons and registered civil partners with a non-resident spouse/partner remain exempt from Capital Gains Tax on transfers of assets to that spouse or partner. This, therefore, provides a very simple method to get capital gains 'offshore'.

Note, however, that any capital gains realised by a non-resident may become liable to UK Capital Gains Tax if that person resumes UK residence after a period of absence of less than five complete UK tax years. (For example, a person resuming UK residence during 2006/2007, having only been non-UK Resident since May 2001.)

For **unmarried** couples, getting gains 'offshore' is not so easy, especially since the hold over reliefs described in Chapter 4 are not available when the transferee is non-UK Resident.

Non-resident partners will remain liable for UK Income Tax on any UK-source income. In many cases they will, however, continue to be eligible for their own £4,895 personal allowance.

A non-resident partner will not generally have to pay UK income tax on *foreign* income. However, a UK Resident may continue to be taxed on such income where it is derived from assets transferred to the non-UK Resident partner.

11.3   ESTABLISHING A PARTNER'S DOMICILE

Later in this chapter, we will look at the enormous tax saving potential where one member of a couple is non-UK Domiciled for Income Tax and Capital Gains Tax purposes.

Before that, however, we need to look at how a person's Domicile is established.

In essence, your 'Domicile' is the country which you consider to be your permanent home.

This does not necessarily equate to your country of birth, nor to the country in which you happen to be living at present.

Furthermore, 'Domicile' should not be confused with residence, which is a far more transitory concept.

Domicile of Origin

At birth, each person acquires the domicile of the person on whom they are legally dependent at that time. That person will, in most cases, be their father but it is their mother if:

- Their father is dead at the time of their birth, or
- Their parents are both alive, but living apart, and they have a home with their mother, but do not have a home with their father.

The domicile which you acquire at birth is known as your 'Domicile of Origin'.

Domicile of Choice

In most cases, a person's Domicile of Origin remains their Domicile for the rest of their life.

This Domicile can only be changed to a 'Domicile of Choice' through permanent emigration (and, in this case, I _mean_ permanent).

Acquiring a new domicile for tax purposes as a 'Domicile of Choice' can be very difficult to prove. This is both good news and bad news since it cuts both ways and Revenue & Customs have had just as much difficulty proving that a taxpayer has acquired the UK as their Domicile of Choice as taxpayers have had in proving that they have acquired a Domicile somewhere else.

As far as this guide is concerned, however, we are primarily concerned with the situation where one of the members of a couple already has a non-UK Domicile of Origin.

11.4   RETAINING A DOMICILE OF ORIGIN

If you are lucky enough to have a non-UK Domicile of *Origin* it is far, far, easier to retain this as your Domicile than it is to acquire a Domicile of *Choice.*

As stated above, it is very difficult for Revenue & Customs to prove that an individual has acquired a new Domicile of choice.

This is especially true if you state that it is your intention to return to your country of origin one day.

In this case, an 'intention' does not necessarily have to be backed up by action, although it is wise to avoid any completely contradictory actions.

Example

Anita was born in Denmark, of Danish parents. She has, however, lived in the UK for over 40 years, having moved here in her early twenties. Despite this, she has always stated that she intends to return 'home' before she dies.

Anita remains domiciled in Denmark.

If one member of a couple is lucky enough to be non-UK domiciled, it is wise for them to establish this fact by completing the appropriate parts of the 'Non-Resident' supplementary pages to their tax return. (Despite its name, this supplement also covers taxpayers who are UK resident but non-UK domiciled.)

It is sensible to do this as soon as possible, even if they have no foreign-source income or gains yet.

196

Following this, the non-domiciled partner will most likely be sent a form 'DOM 1' to complete in order to confirm their non-domiciled status. The key point here is for them to confirm that they do not intend to remain in the UK permanently, i.e. until their death. Any lesser period, such as 'until retirement' or 'until my husband passes away' is, however, acceptable, even if this is still likely to be the majority of their remaining life.

It may also be worth the non-UK domiciled partner buying a grave plot in the country which is their domicile of origin. This would be seen as a very strong indication of their intention to return to that country at some future date.

11.5   DOMICILE AND MARRIAGE OR REGISTRATION

Marriage does not affect a man's domicile and it never has.

For women married on or after 1st January 1974, marriage again has no affect on their domicile.

Likewise, registration of a civil partnership will have no effect on either partner's domicile.

For women married before 1st January 1974, the position is as follows:

- **Non-US Nationals:** A woman married before 1st January 1974 adopted her husband's domicile at the date of marriage. If this changed at any time before 1st January 1974, and they were still married and not legally separated at that time, then her domicile will have changed with his. The woman then continues to have the same domicile as she had on 1st January 1974 unless she subsequently adopted a new domicile of choice.

- **US Nationals:** The domicile of a woman who is a US National is unaffected by marriage.

11.6   TAX PLANNING WITH NON-DOMICILED PARTNERS

So why is it a good thing to have a non-UK domicile?

A non-domiciled partner will not be liable for UK tax on any overseas income or capital gains unless and until they bring the relevant funds back to the UK.

So if one member of a couple is non-UK Domiciled, any income or capital gains derived from that partner's overseas assets can remain free from UK tax as long as the income, or the relevant sales proceeds, are kept offshore.

Remember also that the 'deemed domicile' after 17 years of residence in the UK (see section 10.2) applies only for Inheritance Tax purposes and does not affect the non-domiciled partner's Income Tax or Capital Gains Tax position.

If one partner is non-UK domiciled their ability to invest abroad free of UK Income Tax and Capital Gains Tax (as long as they keep the funds offshore) should continue regardless of how long they live in the UK.

The appropriate strategy is therefore pretty obvious. Any overseas investments should be made by the non-UK Domiciled partner whenever possible.

Where the couple are married or in a registered civil partnership, any transfers to the non-UK Domiciled spouse or partner will continue to be exempt from Capital Gains Tax in the usual way.

Furthermore, hold over relief (see Chapter 4) is still available as long as the transferee, though non-UK Domiciled, remains UK Resident.

It is, however, far better for the non-UK Domiciled partner to make the overseas investments in the first place, as any transfers of assets to them could be subject to the anti-avoidance legislation referred to in section 11.1, resulting in additional Income Tax liabilities for the UK-Domiciled partner.

The second key point, of course, is to keep the income or gains from foreign property offshore.

Keeping funds offshore still permits you to do any of the following:

- Invest funds in the Isle of Man or Channel Islands.
- Hold funds denominated in sterling, but kept offshore.
- Spend the money whilst travelling abroad on business or on holiday.
- Move the funds to a different country outside the UK (but watch out for any local exchange control restrictions).
- Invest in new foreign assets.

Wealth Warning

When doing any of the above, you must take care that the funds never flow via the UK, including any UK bank account.

What About Existing Capital Held Offshore?

Existing capital held offshore before a non-domiciled partner became UK Resident may be brought into the UK without generating any tax charges.

Tax Tip

Have the interest on any such existing capital paid into a separate account.

The 'capital' can then be safely brought into the UK, without causing a taxable remittance of offshore income to the UK.

11.6 FOREIGN TAXES

Where a partner is non-resident or non-domiciled they will probably be subject to taxation in another country.

There is no point, therefore, in simply adopting strategies to minimise your UK taxation without taking the possible foreign tax consequences into account.

You will also need to consider local taxation in the country where the partner is Resident or Domiciled and try to achieve a solution which optimises your overall tax burden, UK and foreign, as a couple.

Chapter 12

Other Legal And Financial Issues

12.1 SCOPE OF THIS CHAPTER

This guide is primarily concerned with tax planning.

There are a number of matters, however, which are highly relevant to the financial affairs of a couple and are therefore worthy of a brief mention.

Where these matters apply to you own circumstances, I would urge you to seek the appropriate professional advice.

12.2 WILLS AND INTESTACY

The first important point to note is that marriage or registration of a civil partnership invalidates any previous will you have made.

It is therefore sensible for the parties to prepare new wills immediately following the marriage or registration.

In the absence of a valid will, the laws of intestacy will operate to determine who inherits your estate.

Whilst the laws of intestacy can usually be expected to provide some level of protection to a spouse or registered civil partner, they will provide nothing for a partner in an unmarried couple.

A will is therefore extra important when you wish to protect your unmarried partner.

Even for married couples and registered civil partnerships, however, the intestacy laws may not operate in the manner you might wish, or even expect, and will also often have an adverse effect for Inheritance Tax purposes.

Intestacy laws also operate differently in England and Wales, Scotland or Northern Ireland.

To protect your partner, therefore, it is essential to make a will.

12.3   BUSINESS PARTNERSHIPS – SOME LEGAL ISSUES

Business partners have 'joint and several liability' for the liabilities of the business partnership.

What this means is that if your business partner goes bankrupt, dies in poverty or disappears off the face of the earth with all the business assets, the business partnership's creditors have the right to demand full payment of all sums due from you. Many a businessman or woman has lost everything they owned under these circumstances.

Often therefore, despite some of the tax planning advantages of bringing their relationship partner into the business partnership, the partner in business has chosen not to do so, in order to be able to protect the couple's personal assets.

Those personal assets can, of course, be kept in the name of the non-business partner in the couple and are thus free from the commercial risks of the business partnership.

Many others choose to form limited liability companies for the same reason.

Since the year 2000, however, there has also been the option to form a 'Limited Liability Partnership'. This type of business vehicle combines the tax advantages of a partnership with the limited liability protection of a company.

In most cases now it will make sense for a couple wishing to form a business partnership together to do so by means of a Limited Liability Partnership.

A Limited Liability Partnership has legal status in UK law as a person in its own right and can therefore enter binding contracts and own property.

A traditional style partnership in England & Wales is not a legal entity in its own right and cannot hold property. A Scottish partnership, however, has always been a separate legal entity able to own property.

12.4 STATE PENSION ENTITLEMENT

In Chapter 3, we considered the benefits of paying a partner a small salary.

Although a salary not exceeding the personal allowance should not result in any National Insurance Contribution liabilities for either the employee partner or the employer partner any salary which exceeds the 'lower earnings limit' will nevertheless preserve the employee's state pension entitlement.

The 'lower earnings limit' for 2005/2006 is £4,264.

This is why it is worth putting up with the bureaucracy of registering as an employer under the PAYE system, as only by doing this will you establish your partner's state pension entitlement.

You can also preserve your partner's state pension entitlement if you manage to ensure that they receive sufficient self-employment income to pay Class 2 National Insurance Contributions.

Both of these methods are considerably cheaper than paying voluntary Class 3 National Insurance Contributions, which are currently paid at the rate of £7.35 per week.

Appendix A

TAX RATES AND ALLOWANCES
2003/2004 TO 2005/2006

	Rates	Bands, allowances, etc.		
		2003/2004	**2004/2005**	**2005/2006**
		£	£	£
Income Tax				
Personal allowance		4,615	4,745	4,895
Starting rate	10%	1,960	2,020	2,090
Basic rate	22%	28,540	29,380	30,310
Higher rate on over	40%	30,500	31,400	32,400
National Insurance Contributions				
Class 2 – per week		2.00	2.05	2.10
Small earnings exception		4,095	4,215	4,345
Class 3 – per week		6.95	7.15	7.35
Class 4:				
Lower profits limit		4,615	4,745	4,895
Upper profits limit	8%	30,940	31,720	32,760
Thereafter	1%			
Capital Gains Tax				
Annual exemption:				
Individuals		7,900	8,200	8,500
Trusts		3,950	4,100	4,250
Inheritance Tax				
Nil Rate Band Threshold		255,000	263,000	275,000
(also set at £285,000 for 2006/2007 and £300,000 for 2007/2008)				
Annual Exemption		3,000	3,000	3,000
Small Gifts Exemption		250	250	250
Pensioners, etc				
Age allowance: 65 –74		6,610	6,830	7,090
Age allowance: 75 & over		6,720	6,950	7,220
MCA: born before 6/4/35		5,565	5,725	5,905
MCA: 75 & over		5,635	5,795	5,975
MCA minimum		2,150	2,210	2,280
Income limit		18,300	18,900	19,500

Appendix B

ILLUSTRATIVE FUTURE TAX RATES

The estimated future tax rates and allowances used for illustrative purposes in the examples in this guide have been calculated using the assumptions set out in section 1.4.

The estimated rates and allowances derived under those assumptions are as follows:

	Rates	Bands, allowances, etc.			
		2006/2007	**2007/2008**	**2008/2009**	**2009/2010**
		£	**£**	**£**	**£**
Income tax					
Personal allowance		£5,025	£5,155	£5,285	£5,425
Starting rate	10%	£2,150	£2,210	£2,270	£2,330
Basic rate	22%	£31,150	£31,990	£32,830	£33,670
Higher rate on over	40%	£33,300	£34,200	£35,100	£36,000
National Insurance Contributions					
Class 2 - per week		£2.15	£2.20	£2.25	£2.30
Small earnings exception		£4,455	£4,575	£4,695	£4,815
Class 3 - per week		£7.55	£7.75	£7.95	£8.15
Class 4:					
Lower profits limit		£5,025	£5,155	£5,285	£5,425
Upper profits limit	8%	£33,580	£34,420	£35,290	£36,180
Thereafter	1%				
Capital Gains Tax					
Annual exemption:					
Individuals		£8,800	£9,100	£9,400	£9,700
Trusts		£4,400	£4,550	£4,700	£4,850
Inheritance Tax					
Nil Rate Band Threshold		£285,000	£300,000	£308,000	£316,000
Pensioners, etc.					
Age allowance: 65 to 74		£7,270	£7,460	£7,650	£7,850
Age allowance: 75 & over		£7,410	£7,600	£7,790	£7,990
MCA: born before 6/4/35		£6,055	£6,215	£6,375	£6,535
MCA: 75 & over		£6,125	£6,285	£6,445	£6,615
MCA minimum		£2,340	£2,400	£2,460	£2,530
Income limit		£20,000	£20,500	£21,100	£21,700
Blind Person's Allowance		£1,660	£1,710	£1,760	£1,810

Appendix C

CONNECTED PERSONS

Connected persons include the following:

Generally

- Husband or wife
- Registered Civil Partner (from 5th December 2005)
- Mother, father or remoter ancestor
- Son, daughter or remoter descendant
- Brother or sister
- Mother-in-law, father-in-law, son-in-law, daughter-in-law, brother-in-law or sister-in-law
- Mother, father, son, daughter, brother or sister of your registered civil partner (from 5th December 2005)
- Business partners
- Companies under the control of the other party to the transaction or of any of his/her relatives as above
- Trustees of a trust where the other party to the transaction, or any of his/her relatives as above, is a beneficiary

Additionally, for the purposes of the pre-owned asset charge only (see section 4.11)

- Aunts and Uncles
- Nephews and Nieces
- Companies under the control of any of these relatives
- Trustees of a trust where any of these relatives is a beneficiary

Appendix D

INDEXATION RELIEF RATES

%'s applying to disposals made by individuals after 5ᵗʰ April 1998 of assets acquired (or enhancement expenditure incurred) during:

Month of expenditure	Index'n Rate	Month of expenditure	Index'n Rate
March 1982 or earlier	104.7%	July-85	70.7%
April-82	100.6%	August-85	70.3%
May-82	99.2%	September-85	70.4%
June-82	98.7%	October-85	70.1%
July-82	98.6%	November-85	69.5%
August-82	98.5%	December-85	69.3%
September-82	98.7%	January-86	68.9%
October-82	97.7%	February-86	68.3%
November-82	96.7%	March-86	68.1%
December-82	97.1%	April-86	66.5%
January-83	96.8%	May-86	66.2%
February-83	96.0%	June-86	66.3%
March-83	95.6%	July-86	66.7%
April-83	92.9%	August-86	67.1%
May-83	92.1%	September-86	65.4%
June-83	91.7%	October-86	65.2%
July-83	90.6%	November-86	63.8%
August-83	89.8%	December-86	63.2%
September-83	88.9%	January-87	62.6%
October-83	88.3%	February-87	62.0%
November-83	87.6%	March-87	61.6%
December-83	87.1%	April-87	59.7%
January-84	87.2%	May-87	59.6%
February-84	86.5%	June-87	59.6%
March-84	85.9%	July-87	59.7%
April-84	83.4%	August-87	59.3%
May-84	82.8%	September-87	58.8%
June-84	82.3%	October-87	58.0%
July-84	82.5%	November-87	57.3%
August-84	80.8%	December-87	57.4%
September-84	80.4%	January-88	57.4%
October-84	79.3%	February-88	56.8%
November-84	78.8%	March-88	56.2%
December-84	78.9%	April-88	54.5%
January-85	78.3%	May-88	53.1%
February-85	76.9%	June-88	52.5%
March-85	75.2%	July-88	52.4%
April-85	71.6%	August-88	50.7%
May-85	70.8%	September-88	50.0%
June-85	70.4%	October-88	48.5%

Appendix D (cont'd)

Month of expenditure	Index'n Rate	Month of expenditure	Index'n Rate
November-88	47.8%	September-92	16.6%
December-88	47.4%	October-92	16.2%
January-89	46.5%	November-92	16.4%
February-89	45.4%	December-92	16.8%
March-89	44.8%	January-93	17.9%
April-89	42.3%	February-93	17.1%
May-89	41.4%	March-93	16.7%
June-89	40.9%	April-93	15.6%
July-89	40.8%	May-93	15.2%
August-89	40.4%	June-93	15.3%
September-89	39.5%	July-93	15.6%
October-89	38.4%	August-93	15.1%
November-89	37.2%	September-93	14.6%
December-89	36.9%	October-93	14.7%
January-90	36.1%	November-93	14.8%
February-90	35.3%	December-93	14.6%
March-90	33.9%	January-94	15.1%
April-90	30.0%	February-94	14.4%
May-90	28.8%	March-94	14.1%
June-90	28.3%	April-94	12.8%
July-90	28.2%	May-94	12.4%
August-90	26.9%	June-94	12.4%
September-90	25.8%	July-94	12.9%
October-90	24.8%	August-94	12.4%
November-90	25.1%	September-94	12.1%
December-90	25.2%	October-94	12.0%
January-91	24.9%	November-94	11.9%
February-91	24.2%	December-94	11.4%
March-91	23.7%	January-95	11.4%
April-91	22.2%	February-95	10.7%
May-91	21.8%	March-95	10.2%
June-91	21.3%	April-95	9.1%
July-91	21.5%	May-95	8.7%
August-91	21.3%	June-95	8.5%
September-91	20.8%	July-95	9.1%
October-91	20.4%	August-95	8.5%
November-91	19.9%	September-95	8.0%
December-91	19.8%	October-95	8.5%
January-92	19.9%	November-95	8.5%
February-92	19.3%	December-95	7.9%
March-92	18.9%	January-96	8.3%
April-92	17.1%	February-96	7.8%
May-92	16.7%	March-96	7.3%
June-92	16.7%	April-96	6.6%
July-92	17.1%	May-96	6.3%
August-92	17.1%	June-96	6.3%

Appendix D (cont'd)

Month of expenditure Index'n Rate

Month of expenditure	Index'n Rate
July-96	6.7%
August-96	6.2%
September-96	5.7%
October-96	5.7%
November-96	5.7%
December-96	5.3%
January-97	5.3%
February-97	4.9%
March-97	4.6%
April-97	4.0%
May-97	3.6%
June-97	3.2%
July-97	3.2%
August-97	2.6%
September-97	2.1%
October-97	1.9%
November-97	1.9%
December-97	1.6%
January-98	1.9%
February-98	1.4%
March-98	1.1%
April 1998 or later	0.0%

Appendix E

BUSINESS ASSETS FOR TAPER RELIEF PURPOSES

This Appendix is intended as a brief overview of the classes of assets which may qualify as business assets for taper relief purposes. This is a complex area of tax law and professional advice should be obtained before relying on the assumption that an asset being disposed of will be accepted as a business asset for these purposes.

Note also that the definition of business asset has changed several times since the introduction of taper relief in 1998. Assets which have not been business assets throughout their entire ownership (or the period since 6th April 1998, if the asset was acquired before that date) will not qualify for the full rate of business asset taper relief.

Shares and securities are treated as business assets for taper relief purposes when the company issuing the shares or securities is a qualifying company by reference to the individual making the disposal.

From 6th April 2000, a company is a 'qualifying company' for this purpose under any of the following circumstances:

- Whenever the company is an *unquoted trading company.* (Broadly, this means that, in addition to qualifying as a trading company, the company must also not be listed on any recognised stock exchange.)

- When the company is a *quoted trading company and the individual* claiming the taper relief *is* an *officer* or *employee* of that company or of another company that is a member of the same group of companies or which may reasonably be considered to be part of the same commercial association of companies.

- When the company is a *quoted trading company and the individual* claiming the taper relief *owns* enough shares to enable *at least 5%* of the voting rights in the company to be exercised.

- When ***the individual*** claiming the taper relief is an ***officer or employee*** of the company, or of another company and ***does not have a 'material interest'*** in the company.

  Broadly speaking, this means that the individual concerned, together with any 'connected persons' does not hold, and cannot control, more than 10% of any class of shares in the company.

From 6th April 2004, assets **other than shares and securities** are regarded as business assets for taper relief purposes when they are used for the purposes of a qualifying trade carried on by:

- A sole trader,
- A partnership,
- A trust,
- The estate of a deceased person, or
- A qualifying company (as defined above).

Partnerships only qualify here as long as at least one member of the partnership falls under one of the other headings above.

The trading entity does not need to be in any way connected with the owner of the asset.

Need Affordable & Expert Tax Planning Help?

Try Our Unique Question & Answer Service

The purpose of this guide is to provide you with detailed guidance on Tax Planning strategies for couples.

Ultimately, you may want to take further action or obtain guidance personal to your circumstances.

Taxcafe.co.uk has a unique online tax service that provides access to highly qualified tax professionals at an affordable rate.

No matter how complex your question, we will provide you with some help through this service. The cost is just £69.95.

To find out more go to **www.taxcafe.co.uk** and click the Tax Questions button.

Pay Less Tax!

... with help from Taxcafe's unique tax guides, software

<u>All products available online at **www.taxcafe.co.uk**</u>

- ➤ **How to Avoid Property Tax** - Essential reading for property investors who want to know all the tips and tricks to follow to pay less tax on their property profits.

- ➤ **Retire Rich with a Property Pension** - Everything you need to know about the new property pension rules, including how to buy property at a 40% discount, paid for by the taxman.

- ➤ **Non Resident & Offshore Tax Planning** - How to exploit non-resident tax status to reduce your tax bill, plus advice on using offshore trusts and companies.

- ➤ **Using a Property Company to Save Tax** - How to massively increase your profits by using a property company... plus all the traps to avoid.

- ➤ **How to Avoid Inheritance Tax** - A-Z of inheritance tax planning, with clear explanations and numerous examples. Covers simple and sophisticated tax planning.

- ➤ **How to Avoid Stamp Duty** - Little known but perfectly legal trade secrets to reduce your stamp duty bill when buying or selling property.

- ➢ **Grow Rich with a Property ISA** - Find out how to invest in property tax free with an ISA.

- ➢ **Using a Company to Save Tax** - Everything you need to know about the tax benefits of using a company to run your business.

- ➢ **Bonus vs Dividend** - Shows how shareholder/directors of companies can save thousands in tax by choosing the optimal mix of bonus and dividend.

- ➢ **How to Avoid Tax on Your Stock Market Profits** - How to pay less capital gains tax, income tax and inheritance tax on your stock market investments and dealings.

- ➢ **Selling a Sole Trader Business** - A potential minefield with numerous traps to avoid but significant tax-saving opportunities.

- ➢ **How to Claim Tax Credits** - Even families with higher incomes can make successful tax credit claims. This guide shows how much you can claim and how to go about it.

- ➢ **Property Capital Gains Tax Calculator** - Unique software that performs complex capital gains tax calculations in seconds.

Disclaimer

1. Please note that this Tax Guide is intended as general guidance only for individual readers and does NOT constitute accountancy, tax, investment or other professional advice. Taxcafe UK Limited accepts no responsibility or liability for loss which may arise from reliance on information contained in this Tax Guide.

2. Please note that tax legislation, the law and practices by government and regulatory authorities (e.g. the Inland Revenue) are constantly changing and the information contained in this Tax Guide is only correct as at the date of publication. We therefore recommend that for accountancy, tax, investment or other professional advice, you consult a suitably qualified accountant, tax specialist, independent financial adviser, or other professional adviser. Please also note that your personal circumstances may vary from the general examples given in this Tax Guide and your professional adviser will be able to give specific advice based on your personal circumstances.

3. This Tax Guide covers UK taxation only and any references to 'tax' or 'taxation' in this Tax Guide, unless the contrary is expressly stated, refers to UK taxation only. Please note that references to the 'UK' do not include the Channel Islands or the Isle of Man. Foreign tax implications are beyond the scope of this Tax Guide.

4. Whilst in an effort to be helpful, this Tax Guide may refer to general guidance on matters other than UK taxation, Taxcafe UK Limited are not experts in these matters and do not accept any responsibility or liability for loss which may arise from reliance on such information contained in this Tax Guide.

5. Please note that Taxcafe UK Limited has relied wholly on the expertise of the author in the preparation of the content of this Tax Guide. The author is not an employee of Taxcafe UK Limited but has been selected by Taxcafe UK Limited using reasonable care and skill to write the content of this Tax Guide.

6. For the purposes of clause 2 above, the date of publication of this guide is 15ᵗ November 2005.

Printed in the United Kingdom
by Lightning Source UK Ltd.
107466UKS00002B/67-204

9 781904 608325